Pelican Books

Understanding Company Financial Statements

R. H. Parker was born in North Walsham, Norfolk, in 1932. He read
Economics at University College, London, from 1951 to 1954. He then
served three years' articles in the City of London before becoming a
member of the Institute of Chartered Accountants in England and Wales
in 1958. Since then he has practised accounting and taught at
universities and business schools in Australia, Britain, France and
Nigeria. He is the author of *Management Accounting: An Historical
Perspective* (1969) and *Readings in Accounting and Business Research
1970–1977* (1978); joint author of *Topics in Business Finance and
Accounting* (1964), *Accounting in Scotland: A Historical Bibliography*
(2nd edition, 1976); *Accounting Thought and Education: Six English Pioneers* (1980) and
Comparative International Accounting (1981); editor of *British Accountants: A
Biographical Sourcebook* (1980) and *Bibliographies for Accounting Historians* (1980);
co-editor of *Readings in the Concept and Measurement of Income* (1969) and *The Evolution
of Corporate Financial Reporting* (1979); and has published numerous articles in
accounting and financial journals.

Since 1976 R. H. Parker has been Professor of Accountancy at the
University of Exeter. He is editor of *Accounting and Business Research*,
published by the Institute of Chartered Accountants in England and
Wales. His main professional interests are in the international,
comparative and historical aspects of accounting.

R. H. Parker   **Understanding
Company
Financial
Statements**

 Penguin Books

For Theresa and Michael

Acknowledgements

For 'The Hardship of Accounting' from *The Poetry of Robert Frost*, edited by Edward Connery Lathem, quoted on p. 40: to the Estate of Robert Frost, Edward Connery Lathem and to Jonathan Cape Ltd. Copyright 1936 by Robert Frost. Copyright © 1964 by Lesley Frost Ballantine. Copyright © 1969 by Holt, Rinehart & Winston, Inc. Reprinted by permission of Holt, Rinehart & Winston, Inc.

Penguin Books Ltd, Harmondsworth, Middlesex, England
Viking Penguin Inc., 40 West 23rd Street, New York, New York 10010, U.S.A.
Penguin Books Australia Ltd, Ringwood, Victoria, Australia
Penguin Books Canada Ltd, 2801 John Street, Markham, Ontario, Canada L3R 1B4
Penguin Books (N.Z.) Ltd, 182–190 Wairau Road, Auckland 10, New Zealand

First published in Pelican Books 1972
Reprinted 1973, 1975, 1976, 1977, 1979
Second edition 1982
Reprinted 1983, 1985

Copyright © R. H. Parker, 1972, 1982
All rights reserved

Made and printed in Great Britain by
Richard Clay (The Chaucer Press) Ltd, Bungay, Suffolk
Filmset in Monophoto Ehrhardt by
Northumberland Press Ltd, Gateshead, Tyne and Wear

Contents

Preface to the Second Edition

An eminent company lawyer has written of the published financial statements of companies that: 'To the average investor or creditor – "the man on the Clapham omnibus" – they are cryptograms which he is incapable of solving.'* This small book is an attempt to make the task easier. It is written for the general reader and the first-year student, not for my fellow accountants, and does not pretend to be more than an elementary introduction to a difficult subject. No previous knowledge is assumed. The emphasis is on analysis and interpretation rather than accounting techniques. Special attention has been paid to making the language of accounting and finance intelligible to the layman.

The first edition of this book was published in 1972. The second retains the general approach of the first but the pace of change has been so fast that almost every page has had to be rewritten. The provisions of the Companies Act 1980 have been incorporated but not those of the Companies Act 1981.

I am greatly indebted to British Vita Company Ltd for allowing me to reprint its 1979 annual report and its 1980 interim report. I am grateful to the company's directors and auditors, to my colleague Mr C. W. Nobes, and to many others for valuable comments on previous drafts of the manuscript, but any errors and misinterpretations that may remain are, of course, my responsibility.

Over the years Mrs E. Ibbotson, Mrs H. Ireland and Mrs M. Baldwin have typed more versions of this book than they or I care to remember. My thanks to them also.

---

*Gower, Cronin, Easson and Wedderburn, *Gower's Principles of Modern Company Law* (Stevens, 4th edn, 1979), p. 507.

1. Companies and their Reports

In sooth a goodly company

REV. RICHARD HARRIS BARHAM, *The Jackdaw of Rheims*

THE PURPOSE AND DESIGN OF THIS BOOK

The purpose of this book is to show the reader how to understand, analyse and interpret the reports sent by companies to their shareholders, and more especially the financial statements contained therein. In order to do this, we shall look in detail at the 1979 report of the British Vita group. We shall also refer occasionally to British Vita's 1978 and earlier reports and to the reports of other companies.

In this first chapter we survey in general terms the contents of a company annual report and look briefly at the nature and constitution of the limited liability company. Chapter 2 describes the various financial statements and introduces many important financial and accounting concepts. This is a vital chapter, providing the basis for the analysis which appears later in the book. Chapter 3 explains as briefly as possible the nature of company taxation and the function of the auditors. Chapter 4 deals with accounting standards and the effect of inflation on accounting. Chapter 5 describes certain tools of analysis. Chapter 6 is concerned with profitability and return on investment, chapter 7 with liquidity and cash flows, and chapter 8 with sources of funds and capital structure. Chapter 9 summarizes the whole book.

Finance and accounting are specialist subjects. This does not mean that they need remain incomprehensible to the layman. It does mean, however, that technical terms cannot entirely be avoided. One would not, after all, learn to drive a car without learning words such as 'clutch' and 'accelerator'. In order to make the learning process as painless as possible, all technical terms are explained as they are introduced and a glossary is provided for reference (Appendix B). It is hoped that some readers will want to know more about finance and accounting after reading this book. For such readers the references given in chapter 9 should be useful.

CONTENTS OF A COMPANY ANNUAL REPORT

The 1979 annual report and accounts of British Vita Company Ltd are reproduced as Appendix C by kind permission of the company. The original has a page size about twice that of the reproduction. British Vita's report has been chosen for three reasons: the company has made a real effort to make its financial statements intelligible to the non-specialist; the information it provides on a number of matters is fuller than that provided by many companies; and, finally, because it is not too large a company (group sales in 1979 of £73·3 million) its report is not so complicated as to be unsuitable for detailed study in an introductory book of this kind.

The content of British Vita's report is typical of that of most companies. To get some idea of this content it is worth leafing quickly through it.

What is the British Vita group and what do the member companies of it do? The group's own succinct description of itself is that the companies in the group are international leaders in foams, fibres, fabrics and rubber technology. The principal activities listed in the directors' report (Appendix C, p. 8) are:

the manufacture of cellular foams, synthetic fibre fillings, rubber and plastic compounds, precision rubber mouldings and fabrications, coated fabrics, adhesives and a range of consumer products. Service activities include haulage contracting, merchanting and property management.

Page 6 on group operations gives further details.

British Vita Company Ltd of Middleton near Manchester is the parent company of the group. There are eight wholly owned subsidiaries operating in England, as well as four European subsidiaries and four African subsidiaries (p. 24), in some of which there are minority shareholdings. The group also has numerous associated companies (p. 25).

Turning back to the beginning of the report, we find first of all the results for 1979 (with comparative figures for 1978) 'at a glance', i.e. in summarized form (p. 1). This is followed by the chairman's review (pp. 2 and 3). Such a review, though not required by law, is published by almost all companies listed on the Stock Exchange. The content varies considerably. That of British Vita for 1979 looks both at the immediate past and at prospects for the future. Research has shown that this is one of the most widely read sections of an annual report.

The next two pages are more formal. Page 4 gives the names of the directors, the secretary, the auditors and the principal bankers. The company's official address ('registered office') is given, as is also that of the 'transfer office' (where transfers of the company's shares are handled). Page 5 gives notice of the annual general meeting of the shareholders of the company. Every company must by law hold such a meeting once a year, with an interval of not more than fifteen months between meetings.

The business of the meeting is very formal:

   to receive and consider the accounts and reports of the directors and auditors for the year ended 31 December 1979;

   to confirm the dividends paid and to declare a final dividend on the ordinary shares (dividends are recommended by directors but approved and declared by the shareholders);

   to re-elect directors;

   to re-appoint the auditors and authorize the directors to fix their remuneration;

   to transact any other ordinary business.

Page 6 on group operations has already been looked at. Page 7 gives details of the effect on the group of the acquisition of Vita-tex Ltd, a company which joined the group on 5 February 1980. Both these pages are published voluntarily.

The next item is the directors' report (pp. 8–12), a statutory document whose contents are largely determined by law (there is a summary of the legal requirements in the Glossary). The main topics dealt with in British Vita's report are profit and dividends, principal activities, analysis of turnover and trading profit, subsidiary companies, associated companies, fixed assets, finance, a subsequent or post-balance sheet event (the acquisition of Vita-tex), directors' and other interests, employee share options, ordinary share capital, close company provisions, personnel, donations and auditors.

Page 13 of the report gives summary financial information for the last five years. Page 14 contains the report of the auditors (see chapter 3) and page 15 lists the accounting policies of the group (see chapter 4).

There now follows the most important and, for many, the most difficult section of the report: the financial statements. These consist of a group profit and loss account, two balance sheets (one for the group and one for the parent company), several pages of notes, current cost accounts, a statement of source and application of funds, and a statement of value added. Details are also given of subsidiary and associated companies (pp. 24 and 25) and there is some shareholding information on page 30. All of these will be looked at in detail later. For the moment it is enough to note that the group profit and loss account and the statement of value added show the results of the operations of the British Vita *group of companies* for the *year ended* 31 December 1979; the group balance sheet shows the financial position of the *group as at* 31 December 1979; the parent balance sheet shows the financial position of *the parent company only as at* 31 December 1979; and the statement of source and application of funds shows the changes in the assets and liabilities of the *group during the year ended* 31 December 1979. The current cost accounts restate the group profit and loss account and balance sheet in terms of current costs.

USERS OF PUBLISHED ACCOUNTS

Although published financial statements are formally for shareholders only, they are also of great interest to other users. *The Corporate Report*, a discussion paper issued by the Accounting Standards Committee in 1975, classifies these other users as employees, loan creditors, analyst advisers, business contacts, the government and the public. It is British Vita's policy to make its annual report generally available and not to prepare statements specifically aimed at other users, especially as many of its employees are also shareholders. Many companies, however, prepare a special report for the employees. This is sometimes, but not always, distributed with the annual report.

MEMORANDUM AND ARTICLES OF ASSOCIATION

It will be convenient occasionally in this book to refer to two documents known as the Memorandum of Association and the Articles of Association. Every company must have both. The main contents of the memorandum are the name of the company, the situation of the registered office, a list of the objects for which the company has been formed, and a statement that the liability of the members is limited. The list of objects is important since a company cannot do anything which is beyond its powers (*ultra vires*). In practice the problem is avoided by listing every conceivable (and sometimes inconceivable) object that the company is ever likely to have.

The articles are the internal regulations of the company and usually deal with such matters as the rights of particular classes of shares, transfer of shares, powers and duties of directors, accounts, dividends, reserves and quorums for meetings of shareholders and directors. A model set of articles (Table A), which can be adopted in full or in a modified form, is appended to the Companies Act 1948.

CLASSIFICATION OF COMPANIES

In Britain the most important form of business organization is the limited liability company. The chief characteristics of such a company are a corporate personality distinct from that of its owners or shareholders; the limiting of the liability of the shareholders to the amount invested (which is not the case for a sole trader or partnership where personal assets are available to pay business debts); and, in principle at least, a perpetual life: companies are born but they do not have to die of old age.

It was not until 1844 that incorporation became possible other than by the slow and difficult process of a special Act of Parliament or a Royal Charter. It took another eleven years for incorporation by registration to be linked with limited liability by the Limited Liability Act 1855. The foundations of modern British company law (and also that of Australia, Canada, New Zealand, South Africa and many other Commonwealth or former Commonwealth countries) were laid in the Companies Act 1862. The law has been continually revised since, notably in 1908, 1929 and 1948. At the time of writing most of the legislation in force is contained in the Companies Acts 1948, 1967, 1976 and 1980. These will be referred to as the Companies Acts 1948 to 1980. The report of the Company Law Committee 1962 (the Jenkins Report) contains many recommendations which have not yet been made law. The Commission of the European Communities has an active programme of company law harmonization which will increasingly affect British companies (see the section below on company law and the E.E.C.).

At the end of 1979 there were about 727,000 companies registered in Great Britain, of which about 16,000 or 2·2 per cent were 'public' companies and about 711,000 were 'private' companies. In 1979, 66,472 new companies were registered with a nominal capital of £830 million.*

To explain the differences between public and private companies it is necessary to look at the ways in which companies can be classified. As from 1981 a public company is one whose memorandum of association states that it is such, whose name ends with the words 'public limited company' or 'plc' (or optionally 'ccc' for companies registered in Wales) and which has a minimum authorized and allotted share capital, one quarter at least of which has been paid up. The minimum amount is set at present at £50,000. Any company which is not a public company is a private company. A private company is not permitted to issue shares or debentures to the public.

A public company does not *have* to make a public issue of shares or debentures; it simply has the right to do so. Thus only about 2,750 public companies are listed (quoted) on a stock exchange and the division between private and public companies is not the same as that between companies with listed shares and those with unlisted shares. It is a necessary but not a sufficient condition for listing that the company be a public company. British Vita is both a public and a listed company.

All companies must have at least two shareholders; there is no maximum limit. At 27 April 1980, for example, Scottish & Newcastle Breweries Ltd had 33,007 ordinary shareholders.† Not all shareholders

---

* Department of Trade, *Companies in 1979* (H.M.S.O., 1980).

† The distinction between shareholders and stockholders, and between shares and stock, is not of practical importance. The terms are increasingly used interchangeably.

are persons. Given below are estimates of percentages of market value of shareholdings by sector of *beneficial* holder. Since shares can be held by a nominee, the beneficial holder is not necessarily the same as the registered holder of a share.

	1963 %	1969 %	1975 %
Personal sector	56·1	49·5	39·8
Financial companies and institutions	30·4	35·9	48·1
Industrial and commercial companies	5·1	5·4	3·0
Public sector	1·5	2·6	3·6
Overseas sector	7·0	6·6	5·6
	100·0	100·0	100·0

Note: Because of rounding the sum of each column may not add to 100. (*Source:* 'The Ownership of Company Shares. A Survey for 1975' *Studies in Official Statistics* No. 34, H.M.S.O., 1979.)

The features to note are the steady fall in personal sector shareholdings and the steady rise in the holdings of financial companies and institutions (i.e. mainly insurance companies and pension funds).

Companies do not have to disclose shareholder statistics but British Vita has voluntarily done so on p. 30 of its 1979 annual report. As at 31 December 1979, the company had 19,882,712 ordinary shares and 2,741 ordinary shareholders, i.e. the *average* holding was 7,254 shares. In fact 51 per cent of the non-institutional shareholders held 1,000 shares or less and 96 per cent of such shareholders held 10,000 shares or less. Only 9·9 per cent of the shareholders were institutions but they held 58·8 per cent of the shares. The average non-institutional shareholding was 3,320 shares; the average institutional holding was 42,965 shares. Shareholdings of 5 per cent or over must by law be reported to the company.

Companies can take the power, and nearly always do so, to hold shares in other companies. A 'holding company' and a 'subsidiary company' exist where the former is a shareholder of the latter *and* controls the composition of the latter's board of directors; *or* where the former holds more than half in nominal value of the latter's equity share capital. An 'associated company' is one in which 50 per cent or less of the shares are held and over which a significant influence is exercised. It is possible for a subsidiary itself to have subsidiaries. These are the sub-subsidiaries of the first holding company. In the example below, A. Ltd is a holding company, B. Ltd a subsidiary, and C. Ltd a sub-subsidiary.

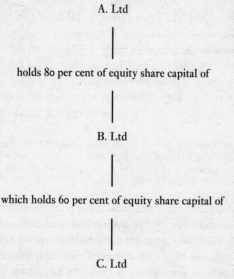

A. Ltd

holds 80 per cent of equity share capital of

B. Ltd

which holds 60 per cent of equity share capital of

C. Ltd

Note that A. Ltd's interest in C. Ltd is only 48 per cent, i.e. 80 per cent of 60 per cent.

Some holding companies exist purely to hold shares in operating subsidiaries. Others, like British Vita Company Ltd, are operating companies as well.

The holding–subsidiary relationship is very common and practically all the annual reports which the reader is likely to be interested in will be those of *groups* of companies. It is possible for subsidiaries to hold shares in each other but the Companies Act 1948 makes it illegal, with minor exceptions, for a subsidiary to hold shares in its holding company, or for any company to purchase its own shares.

The annual reports with which we shall be concerned, then, will be those of groups or sub-groups of companies. The holding company will usually be a public one. Other members of the group will be British public or private companies or companies incorporated overseas.* All those concerned will have share capital. It is worth noting in passing that not all companies do have share capital. Some are 'limited by guarantee', i.e. the members have undertaken to contribute a fixed amount to the assets of the company in the event of its being wound up. The London School of Economics and Political Science is an example. Some companies are even unlimited; since these have the privilege of not publishing their accounts they are not relevant to this book. They are used by professionals who desire corporate form but are not permitted to limit their liability, or by those who value the privilege of non-publication more than the limitation of liability (e.g. the C & A department store). They have become more important since the Companies Act 1967 abolished 'exempt private companies' (essentially family companies exempt from publishing their accounts).

COMPANY LAW AND THE E.E.C.

The E.E.C.'s active programme of company law harmonization means that British company law will be further amended in the near future. The Council of Ministers of the E.E.C. has adopted a series of company law 'directives' which each member state has to incorporate into its own legislation. Many of the provisions of the Companies Act 1980 are a result of the second directive. More important still is the fourth directive. This will be translated into legislation in Britain, through the Companies Act 1981 and will introduce, as well as the distinctions already drawn between public and private companies and listed and unlisted companies, a three-tier classification into large, medium and small companies. Size will be measured by turnover, balance sheet total and number of employees. All listed and some non-listed public companies will be large. Medium companies will be either public or private. Small companies will be private.

The fourth directive will also ensure that the presentation of companies' financial statements will be more standardized than it is at present (see chapters 2 and 4).

---

* The American equivalent of plc and Ltd is Inc. (i.e. incorporated). The nearest French, German and Dutch equivalents to a British public company are a *société anonyme* (S.A.), an *Aktiengesellschaft* (A.G.) and a *Naamloze Venootschap* (N.V.); to our private companies, *société à responsabilité limitée* (S.A.R.L.), *Gesellschaft mit beschränkter Haftung* (G.m.b.H.) and *Besloten Venootschap* (B.V.).

INTERIM REPORTS

Twelve months is a long time to wait for information about the details of the financial progress of a company. It has therefore become increasingly common for major companies to issue unaudited interim reports at half-yearly and sometimes quarterly intervals. Listed companies are required by the Stock Exchange to circularize a half-yearly interim report to shareholders not later than six months from the date of the notice calling an annual general meeting. Companies with exceptionally large numbers of shareholders are allowed to insert such interim reports instead in two leading London newspapers (e.g. the *Financial Times* and *The Times*) or one such newspaper and one provincial newspaper.

British Vita's interim report for the six months ended 30 June 1980 is reproduced in Appendix D. It comprises a chairman's review, a group profit and loss account with comparative figures, and details of earnings and dividends per share.

ANNUAL FINANCIAL STATEMENTS

It is, however, with the annual financial statements that this book is mainly concerned. Now that we have sufficient background information, we can look at them in more detail.

2. The Financial Statements

The statements was interesting but tough

MARK TWAIN, *The Adventures of Huckleberry Finn*, ch. 17

ASSETS, LIABILITIES AND SHAREHOLDERS' FUNDS

At the core of any company's annual report are the financial statements. Those for the British Vita group for the year ended 31 December 1979 are reproduced as Appendix C. We shall start by discussing the 1979 group balance sheet, i.e. the column of figures furthest to the left on page 17 of the appendix. This is a statement of the financial position of British Vita and its subsidiaries at 31 December 1979 as if they were one company.

Traditionally, British companies have had the right to present a balance sheet in any way they please, so long as certain items are either disclosed on the face of the balance sheet or in the notes. As a result of the E.E.C.'s fourth directive on company accounts, balance sheets will be more standardized in form in the future. All balance sheets, however, are built up from three main categories, *viz.* assets, liabilities and shareholders' funds. The relationship between these three items can be looked at either from the point of view of shareholders (a 'proprietary' approach) or from the point of view of the company as a whole (an 'entity' approach). Two forms of the fundamental balance sheet identity can thus be derived:

> *Proprietary:* assets − liabilities = shareholders' funds
> *Entity:* assets = shareholders' funds + liabilities

In less technical language all that is being said is that, firstly, what a company owns *less* what a company owes is equal to the value of the shareholders' funds invested in it and that, secondly, what a company owns is financed partly by the owners (the shareholders) and partly by outsiders (the liabilities). Either way, a balance sheet must, by definition, balance. The useful accounting technique known as double entry (*debits* and *credits*) is based on these same identities (see Appendix A).

As we shall see in the next few sections, the three categories can each be subdivided, e.g. shareholders' funds into share capital and reserves, assets into fixed assets and current assets, and liabilities into current liabilities and long-term (non-current) liabilities.

British Vita has adopted an entity approach and presents its consolidated balance sheet in the following form (App. C, p. 17):

		£,000
Shareholders' Funds (capital and reserves)		24,458
Minority Interests in Subsidiaries*		265
Non-current Liabilities (loans and long term creditors)		8,011
		32,734

		£,000
Fixed Assets		17,012
Associated Companies*		8,615
Deferred Assets*		728
Current Assets	32,507	
deduct Current Liabilities	26,128	
		6,379
		32,734

Explanations of the items marked with an asterisk and of the various items included under each heading are given later in the chapter.

The second important financial statement is the group profit and loss account (App. C, p. 16). It will be noted that whilst a balance sheet is for a particular moment, a profit and loss account (the American phrase is income statement) is for a period, in this case for the year ended 31 December 1979. It shows, from the point of view of the shareholders, the results of the year's activities. The British Vita group made sales ('turnover to external customers') in 1979 of approximately £73·3 million. The trading profit was £6,875,000; after addition of the share of profit of associated companies and deduction of interest this figure rose to £8,928,000 (profit before tax). This was reduced by taxation to £6,826,000 (profit after tax). After allowing for minority interests, the profit attributable to shareholders came to £6,762,000. Out of this amount dividends have been or will be paid to the shareholders amounting altogether to £1,023,000. This leaves £5,739,000 to be retained (ploughed back).

The group profit and loss account is clearly drawn up from the point of view of the shareholders. A rather different view of the same figures is given in the statement of value added on page 29 of Appendix C. Unlike the profit and loss account, this statement is not yet required by law. The philosophy behind a statement of value added is that the group by its activities creates new wealth ('adds value') which is then shared out among the employees, the providers of capital and the government, with a balance being retained to provide for the maintenance and expansion of assets. Statements of value added typically provide some information, e.g. the amount of wages, salaries, pension and social security contributions, which is not given elsewhere in the annual report.

The diagram at the foot of page 29 shows how value added has been applied in 1979:

		%
Personnel (wages, salaries, etc.)		56
Governments (taxation)		16
Providers of capital –		
dividends to shareholders	4	
interest	3	
	—	
		7
Maintenance of assets and expansion –		
depreciation	5	
retained earnings	16	
	—	
		21
		—
		100
		—

It is worth looking more closely at the link between the profit and loss account and the balance sheet. How can a company grow, i.e. how can it increase its assets? Look again at the identity

$$\text{assets} = \text{liabilities} + \text{shareholders' funds}.$$

It is clear that the only ways to increase the assets are to increase the liabilities (i.e. to borrow) or to increase the shareholders' funds. How can a company increase the latter? There are two possibilities: it can issue more shares or it can plough back profits (assuming, of course, it is making some). Ploughing back profits is the simplest but not necessarily the cheapest source of long-term finance for a company. Also, the more a company ploughs back the less, in the short run at least, there will be available for paying dividends.

The sources and uses of funds of a company for a period are shown in a statement of source and application of funds (sometimes known more briefly as a funds statement). In 1979 the British Vita group (App. C, p. 28) generated funds of £9,552,000 from operations. Its uses of funds amounted to £13,024,000. To finance the difference of £3,472,000 it increased its loans by £617,000 and its long-term creditors by £1,225,000, issued shares to the extent of £24,000 and decreased its net cash balances by £1,606,000.

By using simple algebra it is possible to show quite clearly the links between the balance sheet, the profit and loss account and the funds statement. The following symbols will be used:

a = assets	r = revenue (e.g. sales, fees)
l = liabilities	e = expenses other than taxation
c = shareholders' funds	t = taxation
s = share capital	d = dividends
p = retained or ploughed back profits (reserves)	Δ = net increase in

The identity for any balance sheet will then be

$$a = l + c$$

which can be expanded to

$$a = l + s + p \tag{i}$$

The statement of source and application of funds shows the net increase in each item and can therefore be written as

$$\Delta a = \Delta l + \Delta s + \Delta p \tag{ii}$$

The profit and loss account is merely an expansion of the last item on the right-hand side (Δp or net increase in retained profits). The equation is

$$\Delta p = r - e - t - d \tag{iii}$$

Equation (ii) can therefore be expanded to read

$$\Delta a = \Delta l + \Delta s + r - e - t - d \tag{iv}$$

For those who dislike algebra these four equations and their relationships are shown in the following diagrams. It should be noted that the relative proportions of liabilities and shareholders' funds have changed, although, of course, the sum of the two categories must by definition be equal to the assets.

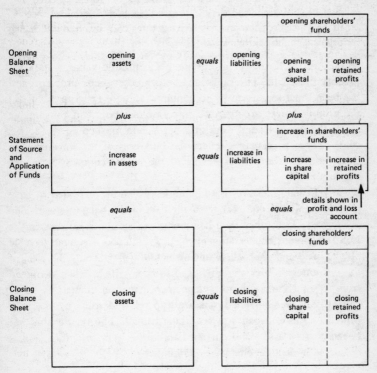

CURRENT ASSETS, CURRENT LIABILITIES AND WORKING CAPITAL

Current assets are those assets which are either in the form of cash or can reasonably be expected to be turned into cash within one year from the date of the balance sheet. The British Vita group at 31 December 1979 had current assets valued at £32,507,000 comprising cash and bank balances of £1,692,000, debtors ('accounts receivable' in U.S. terminology) of £20,572,000, stocks ('inventories') of £10,190,000 and a marketable investment of £53,000. The debtors figure is usually net of an allowance (or provision) for doubtful debts. The figure for stocks may vary according to the rules of valuation adopted. British Vita's policy is set out as follows (App. C, p. 15):

> Stocks have been valued at the lower of cost and net realisable value. The value of finished goods and work in progress has been determined by computations which are appropriate to arriving at the costs involved in bringing the products to their current state.

The use of the lower of cost or net realizable value is standard practice in Britain. The valuation of stock poses many problems and has been much discussed by accountants. In note 15 (App. C, p. 21) the group's stocks are analysed into raw materials and consumable stores (80 per cent) and work in progress and finished goods (20 per cent). These percentages reflect the bulkiness of the finished products, stocks of which, especially of the parent company, are kept at a minimum.

Current liabilities are those liabilities which are expected to have to be paid within one year from the date of the balance sheet. The group at 31 December 1979 had creditors ('accounts payable' in the U.S.) of £20,004,000, taxation owing of £1,426,000, dividends payable of £543,000 and short-term borrowings of £4,155,000. The total of the current liabilities was thus £26,128,000 which, when deducted from the current assets of £32,507,000, gave net current assets of £6,379,000. Net current assets are also referred to as net working capital or (more usually) just working capital. The relationship between current assets and current liabilities is very important and is discussed in detail in chapter 7 on liquidity.

FIXED ASSETS

Fixed assets comprise those assets which are intended for use on a continuing basis for the purpose of the company's activities. Stocks, for example, are not regarded as fixed assets since they are acquired either for immediate resale (e.g. cigarettes as sold by a tobacconist) or as raw materials for use in manufacturing operations, or are the finished or partly finished ('work in progress') results of such operations. It will be seen from the group balance sheet and note 11 (App.

C, p. 20) that the net book values of the fixed assets of the British Vita group at 31 December 1979 were as follows:

	£000
Land and buildings:	
freehold	6,688
long leasehold	1,058
short leasehold	98
	7,844
Plant, equipment and vehicles	9,168
	£17,012

It is worth noting that these would be *current* assets of a company whose business it was to *sell* land, buildings, plant, equipment or vehicles.

Note 11 gives more detailed information, disclosing that some fixed assets are shown at cost and some at a valuation. 'Cost' in accounting has usually meant the historical cost of acquisition or manufacture (if the asset was made by the company for its own use). Historical cost has been favoured by accountants because it is thought to be objective and verifiable by an independent third party (i.e. by an auditor). It can, however, get seriously out of line with current market values, especially in times of inflation. Most accountants therefore now agree that financial statements must be adjusted to take account of changes in specific and/or general prices, but there is still a certain amount of controversy as to how this should be done. The *current* cost of the group's fixed assets is given on page 26 (App. C) as £26,372,000, which is 55 per cent larger than the historical cost figure.

DEPRECIATION

The concept of depreciation means different things to different people, but in an accounting context it normally means spreading the net cost (sometimes after adjustment or revaluation) of a fixed asset over its estimated useful economic life. British Vita explains its policy as follows (App. C, p. 15):

Depreciation has been calculated on the full cost price or revalued amounts at rates estimated to write off the assets over their useful lives, annual reviews being made for obsolescence. The main rates generally in use are:

(a) Freehold buildings (excluding land) – $2\frac{1}{2}\%$ per annum straight line.

(b) Leasehold land and buildings – $2\frac{1}{2}\%$ per annum straight line or over the period of the lease if less than forty years.

(c) Plant (including fixed plant in buildings) – 10% per annum straight line, but, where the estimated useful life of significant plant is short, a higher rate is used.

(d) Motor vehicles – on a reducing balance or straight line basis at rates between 14% and 30% per annum depending on use.

British Vita thus uses both the straight-line (or linear) and the reducing balance methods of depreciation. The straight-line method is the simpler and consists of dividing the cost less estimated scrap value of an asset by the estimated useful life. If, for example, a machine costs £1,200 and is expected to have a scrap value of £130 at the end of an estimated useful life of ten years, then the annual depreciation expense using this method will be £1,070/10 = £107.

As the name implies, the amount of depreciation charged each year under the reducing balance method decreases over the life of the asset. If, for example, a rate of 20 per cent were chosen for the asset which cost £1,200, the annual depreciation charges would be calculated as shown on page 27.

The machine has been written down to its approximate scrap value. The correct percentage can be found by trial and error or by use of the formula:

$$1 - \sqrt[n]{\frac{s}{c}}$$

where n is the number of years, s the estimated scrap value and c the cost. In this case

$$1 - \sqrt[10]{\frac{130}{1200}} = 0 \cdot 2$$

The charging of depreciation simultaneously (1) reduces the recorded amount of the fixed asset, and (2) reduces net profit.

For the year ended 31 December 1979 the group charged against profits £1,536,000 of depreciation. The amounts given for the fixed assets in the group balance sheet are net of all accumulated depreciation, not only that of the current year but of all previous years since the purchase of the assets concerned.

GOODWILL, MINORITY INTEREST AND ASSOCIATED COMPANIES

A company is not just a collection of tangible assets. It is, or should be, a going concern whose total value, by reason of its proven ability to earn profits, is greater than the sum of its parts. It is the difference between the total value and the sum of the parts which constitutes goodwill. It should not be regarded as in any way a fictitious asset: to be valuable an asset does not have to be tangible. Goodwill is, however, very difficult to value objectively and it is for this reason that it very seldom appears in a balance sheet unless it has been purchased, and even then it is often written off quite quickly. This explains why British Vita's group balance sheet does not include any goodwill derived from the balance sheets of the individual companies

		£
Cost		1,200
Year 1	Depreciation 20% of £1,200	240
		960
Year 2	„ 20% of £960	192
		768
Year 3	„ 20% of £768	154
		614
Year 4	„ 20% of £614	123
		491
Year 5	„ 20% of £491	98
		393
Year 6	„ 20% of £393	79
		314
Year 7	„ 20% of £314	63
		251
Year 8	„ 20% of £251	50
		201
Year 9	„ 20% of £201	40
		161
Year 10	„ 20% of £161	32
		£129

in the group. In some group balance sheets, however, an item appears entitled 'goodwill arising on consolidation' or 'goodwill on acquisition'. This represents the excess of the cost of shares in subsidiary companies over the book value of their net tangible assets at the date of acquisition, i.e. the parent company was willing to pay more to purchase a company than the sum of its tangible fixed and net current assets. British Vita writes off goodwill on acquisition to reserves (App. C, p. 15, para. 1 and p. 22, note 20).

Goodwill on consolidation can, by definition, appear only in a group or consolidated balance sheet. It is appropriate at this point to consider the differences between the balance sheet of the British Vita group and of British Vita Company Ltd itself. Apart from the size of the figures, it will be seen that the main differences are that 'minority interests in subsidiaries' appears only in the group balance sheet whilst 'subsidiaries' appears only in the parent company balance sheet.

The item 'subsidiaries' is explained in note 20 (App. C, p. 20) as comprising the cost of the shares (minus amounts written off), less the amounts owed to dormant subsidiaries and plus those owed by operating subsidiaries. All these are eliminated in the group balance sheet and replaced by the underlying assets and liabilities of the subsidiaries. We have already encountered goodwill on acquisition as a balancing figure.

The item 'minority interests in subsidiaries' represents the proportion of the subsidiaries' assets and liabilities which are owned by outside shareholders. It is a separate item which is neither a liability of the group nor part of the parent company's shareholders' funds.

Both the parent company and the group have interests in associated companies. The shares of these are valued at cost in the company's books but this is increased in the group balance sheet to include a proportionate share of their reserves (retained profits) since acquisition. An associated company is one which is not controlled by the parent company but over which the latter exercises a significant influence. The accounting treatment, which clearly differs from that used for a subsidiary, is known as the 'equity method'.

The nature of deferred assets, and especially advance corporation tax recoverable, is explained in chapter 3.

The Companies Acts require the publication of both group and parent balance sheets. The former is by far the more significant.

LOAN CAPITAL

To the extent that a company cannot or does not wish to obtain long-term funds from its shareholders, it must borrow from outsiders. Such borrowings are called loan capital or medium- and long-term debt.

The British Vita group at 31 December 1979 had loans of £6,511,000 and long-term creditors of £1,500,000. Details are given in notes 21 and 22 on page 22 of Appendix C. The group has borrowed both long term (over five years) and medium term (repayable within five years), both in the U.K. and overseas. The proportion of the loans payable within one year has been transferred to short-term borrowings, a current liability.

Loans to companies are sometimes known as debentures, the word 'debenture' simply referring to a document evidencing a long-term borrowing or loan. Debentures are usually, but not necessarily, secured on the assets of the company, in which case they may be known as mortgage debentures. If a company fails in its obligation to pay interest or repay the loan, certain property of the company can be sold in order to provide the necessary funds. The phrase 'unsecured debenture' is unusual, 'unsecured loan' being preferred in practice. 'Debenture stock' means that instead of issuing individual debentures the company has created one loan fund to be divided among a class of lenders, each of whom will receive a debenture stock certificate. Companies may, and often do, make more than one issue of debentures, the terms of issue and, in particular, the rate of interest varying according to the financial circumstances of the time. Such issues may be made at par (i.e. at face value), at a discount (less than face value) or at a premium (more than face value). Issue at a discount increases the effective interest rate payable; issue at a premium (rare) reduces it. Issues are often made at a discount in order to keep the interest rate on the par value (known as the coupon rate) a reasonably round figure, whilst allowing the effective rate to be adjusted more finely.

Debentures and loans may be secured by a fixed charge on a particular asset or by a floating charge on all the assets or particular classes of assets. A floating charge, unlike a fixed charge, allows a company to dispose of the assets charged in the usual course of business without obtaining special permission from the lender. Stock-in-trade is a particularly suitable asset to be charged in this manner. If assets are, or may be, used as security for more than one loan, it is necessary to state the order of priority of the lenders, e.g. debenture stock may be stated to be secured by a *first* floating charge.

Some debentures are irredeemable, i.e. they will never have to be repaid (unless the company is wound up), but most are redeemable. It is common to specify not only the latest date, but also to give the company the power to redeem earlier if it so wishes. This is especially useful if debentures are issued in times of high interest rates and if there is an expectation of lower rates later.

The long-term creditors of British Vita relate to assets bought on hire purchase or for which government grants have been received.

How much loan capital to issue and when and in what form to issue it, are vital matters to any company. We shall look at these problems in chapter 8.

SHARE CAPITAL AND RESERVES

The shareholders' funds section of the group balance sheet is subdivided into share capital and reserves. Further details are given in notes 19 and 20 (App. C, pp. 21 and 22).

Shareholders differ from debentureholders in that they are members (owners) of the company not lenders, in that they receive dividends (a share of the profits) not interest, and in that, except in special circumstances, the cost of their shares will not be repaid to them by their company. Listed shares can of course be sold on a stock exchange, but the company itself is in general forbidden by law from buying back or redeeming its own shares. An exception is the redeemable preference share (see Glossary).

There are two main types of shares: ordinary and preference. The difference between an ordinary shareholder and a preference shareholder is very important. The latter is usually entitled only to a dividend at a fixed rate (4·2 per cent in the case of British Vita) but has priority of repayment in the event of the company being wound up. This is not always so, however, and the exact rights must always be looked up in the company's articles of association. Preference shares may be cumulative or non-cumulative. British Vita's are cumulative, which means that if the company misses a dividend payment it carries it forward to the next year. Any arrears of preference dividends must be shown in a note to the balance sheet. Non-cumulative preference dividends, on the other hand, do not have to be carried forward.

The ordinary shareholder is not entitled to a fixed dividend, the size varying according to the profits made by the company. It can be seen from note 8 (App. C, p. 19) that an interim ordinary dividend of 2·4p per share was paid during 1979 and that a final ordinary dividend of 2·6p is proposed. The total ordinary dividend is thus 5·0p. The par or face value of the ordinary shares is 25p each (App. C, p. 21, note 19) and the total dividend could be described as a dividend of 20 per cent on the par value.

More important to an investor is the relationship between the dividend and the current *market* price of the share. This is known as the dividend yield and is discussed in chapter 8 in the context of earnings yields and price–earnings ratios. For the moment, it should be noted that every share must have a par value* but that this is not necessarily the same as the issue price of the shares or their market price. Shares can be issued at more than their par value: this gives rise to a *share premium*. The British Vita group has a share premium of £16,000 (App. C, p. 22, note 20). A share premium cannot be distributed but it can be used to make a bonus or capitalization issue (see p. 32). Once a share has been issued, its market price fluctuates from day to day in accordance with supply and demand. If the shares can be bought and sold on a stock exchange then the current market price can easily be obtained from the financial pages of a newspaper or from the *Stock Exchange Daily Official List*. The most complete newspaper list is given in the *Financial Times*. The information given in that paper's daily share information service is further discussed in chapter 8.

A company does not have to issue all its shares at once, nor does it have to request full payment on the shares immediately. British Vita has authority to issue, i.e. it has authorized capital of, 28,000,000 ordinary shares of 25p each, and 60,000 4·2 per cent cumulative preference shares of £1 each (App. C, p. 21, note 19). As at 31 December 1979 it had issued 19,882,712 ordinary shares (par value £4,971,000) and 57,000 preference shares (par value £57,000). All the shares are described as being fully paid, that is the company does not have the right to call up any further amounts from the shareholders. They could have been partly paid. For example, a 25p share could

---

* No-par-value shares are common in North America but illegal in the U.K.

be payable 5p on application for the shares, a further 5p on allotment when the directors decide to whom the shares are going to be issued, and the remaining 15p in calls. Thus, in summary, one can distinguish authorized, issued, called-up and paid-up share capital.

A study of note 19 on page 21 (App. C) reveals that during 1979 British Vita increased both its authorized and its issued ordinary share capital, although not by the same amounts. The increase in authorized share capital of £2 million was approved by the shareholders at the annual general meeting held on 11 April 1979. The text of the resolution is given on page 5 of the company's 1978 report. The issued ordinary share capital was increased by £853,000. Details are given on page 12 of the 1979 Directors' Report:

	£000
Capitalization issue	
(3,303,727 shares at 25p each)	826
Issue under share option scheme	
(107,877 shares at 25p each)	27
	853

A capitalization issue is also called a bonus issue, a scrip issue, or, in the United States, a stock dividend. The word 'bonus' is rather misleading as we shall see in chapter 8, where bonus issues are further discussed.

Details of the group's reserves are given in note 20 (App. C, p. 22). The Companies Act 1980 (which did not, of course, apply to British Vita's 1979 financial statements) establishes a distinction between 'distributable' and 'undistributable' reserves. The former comprises realized profits less realized losses; the latter includes such items as share premiums and reserves arising from the revaluation of assets. The British Vita group's total reserves at 31 December 1979 amounted to £19,430,000, the bulk of which were distributable retained profits.

It is very important not to confuse reserves with cash. To say that a company has large reserves is not the same thing as saying that it has plenty of cash. If a company has reserves it must have net assets of equal amount, but these assets may be of any kind (e.g. machinery, stock-in-trade). Thus it is perfectly possible (and often sensible) for a company to have both large reserves and a large bank overdraft. The balance sheet of the British Vita group at 31 December 1979 shows reserves of £19,430,000, bank balances of £1,692,000 and short-term borrowings of £4,155,000.

GROUP PROFIT AND LOSS ACCOUNT AND STATEMENT OF VALUE
ADDED

As already noted, the group profit and loss account and the statement
of value added (App. C, pp. 16 and 29) deal with essentially the same
information but from a different point of view. The former moves
directly from group turnover to trading profit. Note 2 on page 18
gives details of some but not all the intermediate items. Given below
is an expanded profit and loss account making use of all three sources
of information:

	£000	£000	£000
Sales to external customers (turnover)			73,296
Trading profit			6,875
after charging			
Materials and services (excluding taxes)		43,771	
includes:			
Leasing of vehicles and plant	468		
Government grants	(45)		
Auditors' remuneration	90		
Wages, salaries, pension and social			
security contributions (including			
directors' emoluments of £367,000)		16,662	
Depreciation		1,536	
Share of profits of associated companies			3,129
Interest			(1,076)
Profit before tax			8,928
Tax			(2,102)
Profit after tax			6,826
Minority interests			(64)
Profit before extraordinary items			6,762
Extraordinary items			—
Profit attributable to shareholders			6,762
Dividends			(1,023)
Profit retained for year			5,739
Earnings per share:			
Basic			34·1p
Fully diluted			32·2p

Each item in the expanded profit and loss account will now be looked at in more detail.

The first item is group turnover. This, as note 1 on page 18 tells us, represents the net amounts invoiced to customers in respect of goods supplied and services rendered. Value added and sales taxes are excluded. Turnover within the group is not included since this would merely inflate both sales and the purchases. The sales of associated companies are also excluded. Further information about sales can be found in the directors' report (p. 8) and on page 6. Analyses of turnover are provided by product (e.g. cellular foams of £28 million), by market sold to (e.g. furniture 29 per cent) and by geographical area (e.g. £55 million of the goods sold are manufactured in the U.K. This last figure includes an export turnover of £3,392,000.) Exports are required to be disclosed by company law, and the Stock Exchange requires a geographical analysis of turnover, but the remaining information is provided voluntarily.

The statement of value added includes a figure for turnover of £81,173,000 which *includes* value added and sales taxes. If the tax element in this figure (£81,173,000 − £73,296,000 = £7,877,000) is deducted from the materials and services figure in the statement of value added, materials and services *excluding* taxes must presumably be £43,771,000 (£51,648,000 − £7,877,000). This item includes all those costs, apart from wages and salaries, depreciation and interest, which the group has had to incur in order to achieve its turnover. As the law stands at the time of writing only certain items must, by law, be disclosed separately in the published profit and loss account. The complete list is given in the glossary under the heading Profit and Loss Account.

Details of wages and salaries need not at present be disclosed, apart from those on directors' emoluments set out by British Vita in note 2 on page 18.

The nature and accounting treatment of depreciation has already been discussed. In 1979 depreciation (£1,536,000) was 2·1 per cent of group turnover. This, however, ignores the effects of inflation. In the current cost profit and loss account (p. 26), depreciation (£1,536,000 + £1,773,000 = £3,309,000) is 4·5 per cent of turnover. Vehicles and plant may be leased instead of owned (see chapter 8).

Either way the group has the use of them – hence the law also requires disclosure of leasing charges.

Interest payable is analysed, in accordance with the requirements of the Companies Acts, in note 4 on page 18.

The next item is the group share of profits of associated companies. The accounting treatment of associated companies differs, as we have seen, from that of subsidiaries. Like the latter, the appropriate share of profit or loss before tax is brought into the group results and not just dividends received; but unlike the latter it is brought in as one figure, not split into its component parts. British Vita discloses in note 3 on page 18 both its share of the profits of its associated companies (£3,129,000) and dividends receivable from them (£947,000). In the balance sheet, it will be remembered, the underlying assets and liabilities of an associated company are *not* brought in, but instead the cost of the original investment is augmented by a share of the associated company's retained profits since acquisition.

The next item to note in the British Vita group profit and loss account is taxation. Taxation is so important that it is discussed at length in chapter 3.

The profit after tax is not the same as the profit attributable to shareholders. Two more items need to be deducted. These are the share of the profit after tax which is attributable to the minority shareholders in the subsidiary companies in the group (£64,000 in 1979) and the 'extraordinary' items (nil in 1979 but £30,000 in 1978). Standard accounting practice distinguishes between extraordinary items, exceptional items and prior year adjustments. *Extraordinary items* are those which derive from events or transactions outside the ordinary activities of a business and which are both material and expected not to recur frequently or regularly. *Exceptional items* derive from the ordinary activities of the business. *Prior year adjustments* are material adjustments applicable to prior years arising from changes in accounting policies or from the correction of fundamental errors. Several examples of extraordinary items for 1978 can be found in note 6 on page 19.

We have at last reached the profit attributable to shareholders. This amounted to £6,762,000 in 1979. The remainder of the profit and loss account is concerned with the distribution or retention of this sum: £1,023,000 has been or will be distributed; £5,739,000 is to be retained. Details of dividends are given in note 8 on page 19. An interim dividend of £478,000 has already been distributed to the ordinary shareholders. A final dividend of £543,000 is proposed. The preference shareholders receive £2,000.

At the foot of the group profit and loss account a note is given of the earnings per ordinary share both basic and fully diluted. Earnings per share (EPS) is based on earnings per *ordinary* share and *before* extraordinary items. The relevant figure for earnings was thus £6,760,000 in 1979 and £4,887,000 in 1978. EPS is not of interest to preference shareholders since their dividend is fixed irrespective of the level of earnings. The inclusion of extraordinary items would distort year-to-year comparisons.

As at 31 December 1979 there were 19,882,712 shares (p. 30). The EPS calculation is, however, based on the weighted average of ordinary shares in issue during the year, *viz.* 19,847,368 shares (p. 19, note 9). The calculation of basic EPS is thus:

$$\text{Basic EPS} = \frac{6,760,000 \times 100}{19,847,368} \, p = 34 \cdot 1 p$$

The concept of earnings per share is discussed further in chapter 8.

Profit earned needs to be related to investment made and compared, if possible, with the performance of similar companies. Profitability and return on investment form the main subjects of chapter 6.

STATEMENT OF SOURCE AND APPLICATION OF FUNDS (FUNDS STATEMENT)

It will be remembered that a funds statement shows *changes* during the year in assets, liabilities, share capital and retained profits and that the last item is made up of revenues less expenses (including depreciation), less tax, and less dividends. British Vita group's statement of Source and Application of Funds for the year ended 31 December 1979 is given on p. 28 of Appendix C.

In summary terms the sources and applications of funds (arranged in order of importance) were as follows:

	£000	%
Sources		
Total funds generated from operations (mainly composed of profit before tax after adding back depreciation)	9,552	73
Decrease in net cash balances	1,606	12
Increase in long-term creditors	1,225	9
Increase in loans	617	5
Increase in ordinary share capital (but *not* including the capitalization issue)	24	1
	13,024	100
Uses (Applications)		
Purchase of fixed assets	5,284	41
Purchase of new subsidiaries	2,714	21
Tax on profit for the year	2,102	16
Working capital movement excluding cash (i.e. stock + debtors − creditors)	1,599	12
Dividends paid and proposed	1,023	8
Other uses	302	2
	13,024	100

By far the most important source of funds for the British Vita group in 1979 was that generated from its own operations (73 per cent). Less important were a decrease in cash balances (12 per cent) and increases in long-term creditors (9 per cent) and loans (5 per cent). The increase in ordinary share capital was a result of the share option scheme and not really an attempt to raise funds for expansion. The capitalization is excluded as a source; it did not raise any *new* funds.

The most important uses of funds were the purchase of fixed assets (41 per cent), the purchase of new subsidiaries (21 per cent), tax (16 per cent), the net increase in working capital (12 per cent) and dividends (8 per cent). The assets and liabilities acquired on the purchase of new subsidiaries are given in a note to the funds statement. The tax and dividend figures are identical to those in the group profit and loss account. Some companies show in the funds statement tax *paid* and dividends *paid*; these figures will be different from tax *payable* on the profit for the year and this year's dividends paid and *proposed*.

DEPRECIATION AS A 'SOURCE' OF FUNDS

Depreciation is sometimes described as a 'source' of funds. It will be noted that the British Vita group has been careful not to do this. The depreciation for the year of £1,536,000 is shown in the statement of source and application of funds as the largest of several 'adjustments for items not involving the movement of funds'.

Depreciation is in fact neither a source nor an application (use) of funds. The use of funds obviously took place when the fixed asset was originally bought. It would be double counting to regard each year's depreciation as a further use, and the relevant profit figure in the statement of source and application of funds is therefore *profit before charging depreciation* (but after charging wages, etc.). But the same arithmetical result can be reached by adding back depreciation to profit *after* charging depreciation. This is quite commonly done, but it should not mislead us into thinking that funds can be obtained merely by increasing the depreciation charge in the books.* If, for example, British Vita group's depreciation had been £1,546,000 instead of £1,536,000, then its profits before taxation would have been £8,918,000 instead of £8,928,000 and its total sources of funds would have remained unchanged.

CASH FLOW

Cash flow is a term popular with financial analysts rather than accountants. It is often used rather imprecisely but is usually defined as net profit plus depreciation and other items not involving the movement of funds. A more accurate name for cash flow in this sense is 'total funds generated from operations'. A study of British Vita's source and application of funds statement should make it clear why this figure is different from the change in net cash balances.

EVENTS AFTER THE BALANCE SHEET DATE

Important events may sometimes take place between the date of the balance sheet (e.g. 31 December 1979) and the date on which the

---

* The change in the depreciation charge would not affect the tax payable (see chapter 3 below).

balance sheet is approved by the board of directors for publication (e.g. 14 March 1980). British Vita, for example, reports the acquisition on 5 February 1980 of a majority of the shares of Vita-tex Ltd (App. C, p. 10). This extension of the group's activities is something of which readers of the annual report need to be made aware. Since it does not provide additional evidence of conditions existing at the balance sheet date it is technically known as a 'non-adjusting event'. An example of an 'adjusting event', one which would require the financial statements to be altered if the amount was material, is the insolvency of a debtor as at the date of the balance sheet which only becomes known after the financial statements have been approved by the board.

CONTINGENCIES AND COMMITMENTS

Company law requires the disclosure in the notes of contingent liabilities and capital commitments.

A contingency is a condition which exists at the balance sheet date, the outcome of which will be confirmed only on the occurrence or non-occurrence of one or more uncertain events. British Vita (p. 23, note 25) has a number of contingent liabilities; it has, for example, guaranteed certain of the overdrafts and third party liabilities of certain of its subsidiaries. As from 1980, standard accounting practice extends the requirement to contingent assets.

As required by law, British Vita discloses in note 26 its commitments for capital expenditure not provided for in the accounts and the capital expenditure authorized by the directors but not contracted for. The reader of the annual report thus has knowledge of important projected cash outlays in the forthcoming period.

3. Taxation and Audit

Taxation?
Wherein? And what taxation? My Lord Cardinal,
You that are blamed alike with us,
Know you of this taxation?

WILLIAM SHAKESPEARE, *King Henry the Eighth*, I. ii

Never ask of money spent
Where the spender thinks it went
Nobody was ever meant
To remember or invent
What he did with every cent

ROBERT FROST, *The Hardship of Accounting*

This short chapter deals briefly with two important matters of which all readers of company reports should have some knowledge – taxation and audit. No attempt will be made to go into either in detail; company taxation in particular can become fearsomely complicated.

TAXATION IN THE ACCOUNTS

There are several references to taxation in British Vita's 1979 annual report and accounts. Taxation provided on the group profit for the year ended 31 December 1979 is stated in the profit and loss account to be £2,102,000, i.e. 24 per cent of the profit before tax of £8,928,000. There are two taxation items in the balance sheets: advance corporation tax (ACT) recoverable (£468,000), included under deferred assets, and taxation (£1,426,000), included as a current liability. The source and application of funds statement also includes the tax on the profit for the year. The taxation figure in the statement of value added is much higher (£4,625,000). This is because it includes taxation of all kinds, not just corporation tax. Further details of the company's tax position are given in Appendix C, notes 5, 14 and 23.

CORPORATION TAX

Companies pay corporation tax, not income tax. Taxable income is
measured very much in the same way as accounting profit, with two
major exceptions which relate to depreciation and the stock element
in cost of goods sold. The corporation tax rate is imposed annually
in arrears for the financial year 1 April to 31 March. The tax is
assessed, however, on the basis of a company's accounting period.
British Vita's accounting period ends, it will be remembered, on
31 December each year. The tax is payable for most companies nine
months after the end of the financial year in which the company's
accounting period ends. The rate of corporation tax can vary. In the
financial year 1979 (i.e. from 1 April 1979 to 31 March 1980) it was
52 per cent. A lower rate applies to small profits.

When a dividend is paid by a company it pays advance corporation
tax (ACT), an advance payment on the corporation tax liability, to
the Inland Revenue. The amount paid depends on the basic rate of
income tax. Shareholders are taxed on the dividend grossed up at
the basic rate, but receive a tax credit which can be set against their
liability to income tax. The following example, which assumes for
simplicity a corporation tax rate of 50 per cent and a basic rate of
income tax of 30 per cent shows how this 'imputation system', as
it is called, works.

Taxable profit	1,000
Corporation tax at 50%	500
Profit after tax	500
Dividend paid	315
Retained profit	185
ACT paid by company (3/7 × £315)	135
The shareholders receive:	
Dividend	315
plus tax credit	135
	450

The dividends paid or proposed are shown in the company's accounts
as the cash amounts received or receivable by the shareholders.

Let us suppose that the shareholder is not a company and holds all the shares. He would be assessed for income tax on £450, not £315. If he pays tax at 30 per cent he can set off his tax credit of £135 against his liability to tax of the same amount. If he pays tax at less than 30 per cent he is entitled to a refund; if he pays at more than 30 per cent he has more to pay. A shareholder which is a company would treat such a dividend as 'franked investment income' and would not be assessed to corporation tax on it. It could pass on the tax credit to its own shareholders.

The company itself can normally (but not always, see below) recover the ACT paid (£135) by setting it off against its liability to corporation tax (£500) on its taxable profits. The difference (£365) is called 'mainstream' corporation tax.

CAPITAL ALLOWANCES AND INVESTMENT INCENTIVES

As already noted in chapter 2, capital allowances differ in amount from the depreciation shown in a company's accounts. The main reason for this is that whilst a company in reporting to its shareholders is interested in calculating profit as accurately as possible, the government is more interested in trying to encourage investment.

The present system of capital allowances is meant to act as an incentive to investment by allowing a very large write-off in the first year of ownership. For machinery and plant (which includes furniture, fixtures and fittings and some motor vehicles), new or second-hand, there is a first-year allowance of 100 per cent of the expenditure. Where a first-year allowance is not available (e.g. ordinary motor cars) there is an annual writing-down allowance on the reducing balance.

For industrial buildings and hotels an initial allowance of 50 per cent currently applies, together with a 4 per cent annual writing-down allowance which begins in the first year and is based on cost. The allowances for an industrial building costing £100,000 would be as follows:

	£	£
Cost		100,000
Year 1 Initial allowance		
50% of £100,000	50,000	
Writing-down allowance		
4% of £100,000	4,000	
		54,000
		46,000
Year 2 Writing-down Allowance		4,000
		42,000
Year 3 Writing-down Allowance		4,000
		38,000
		and so on

There are no capital allowances at all on non-industrial buildings such as retail shops, offices and dwelling-houses.

It is important to note that all the allowances described above operate as deductions in the calculation of taxable income. If the latter is large enough to cover the allowances then their effect is to reduce the company's tax bill by the amount of the allowances multiplied by the corporation tax rate. A company which has no taxable income to offset against the allowances does not benefit at all.

This is not true of government grants. These are not reductions in taxable income but payments of cash to a company by the government. They are thus not dependent on the company making a taxable profit. The receipt of such grants does not affect capital allowances. It is standard accounting practice for grants relating to fixed assets to be credited to profit and loss account over the expected useful life of the asset, *either* by (1) reducing the cost of the acquisition of the fixed asset by the amount of the grant, *or* by (2) treating the amount of the grant as a deferred credit (shown separately in the balance sheet), a portion of which is transferred to revenue annually. Other grants are credited to revenue in the year in which the expenditure to which they relate is charged.

Apart from capital allowances many companies are also entitled to 'stock appreciation relief'. This is a rather rough and ready method of giving taxation relief for that part of the increase in the money value of stock-in-trade which is due to increased prices and not increased volume.

The effect of capital allowances and stock appreciation relief is to create what are known as timing differences and to reduce taxable income in the current year well below the company's profit before tax.

It could be argued that the taxation payable has not been saved but merely 'deferred' to a later year. Clearly, for example, by taking a 100 per cent capital allowance on machinery bought this year the company has deprived itself of any allowances on that machinery in future years. Whether or not a provision should be made for 'deferred taxation' is a matter which has aroused a lot of discussion in the accounting world.

British Vita's policy in this matter is set out on page 15 of Appendix C as follows:

Deferred taxation is accounted for in respect of the taxation effects of all timing differences of a material amount other than those which can be demonstrated with reasonable probability to continue in the future.

Note 23 on page 23 states that applying this accounting policy means that in 1979 no provision is required for deferred taxation. Calculating deferred taxation on what is known as the 'liability method' (i.e. estimating the amount which in various circumstances the company would actually have to pay), the *potential* amount payable by the group is £5,534,000. The size of this figure (23 per cent of the shareholders' funds of £24,458,000) shows how important it is to know how a company has treated deferred taxation.

ACT RECOVERABLE: A DEFERRED ASSET

Included among British Vita's deferred assets is the item 'ACT recoverable' (page 21, note 14). This arises mainly because the ACT which British Vita has to pay on its proposed dividends is payable within the next accounting period (1980) whereas it is recoverable only in 1981. Whilst, therefore, it is clearly a current *liability*, it must be regarded as a *deferred* rather than a current asset. Note 14 also includes other examples of deferred assets.

Where a company has no liability to corporation tax, the ACT is not recoverable and has to be written off. Such a situation may be caused by a combination of low profitability and generous tax allowances, and has meant that for many companies corporation tax has effectively become a tax on dividends rather than on profits.

CAPITAL GAINS TAX

Individuals are taxed not only on their income but also on certain capital gains, i.e. the excess of the price they receive on selling an asset over the price they paid for it. Companies are not liable to capital gains tax on their capital gains, but 15/26 of them are instead charged to corporation tax. The effect of this is that the gain is charged at 30 per cent.

Tax does not become payable when an asset is revalued unless it is sold. Since fixed assets are held for use rather than sale, it is not the practice to make provision for the tax which would arise if the assets were sold for the revalued amount (see British Vita's note 11, p. 20).

If a gain is made from selling an asset owned on 6 April 1965, only that part of the gain related to the period from 6 April 1965 to the date of sale is taxable. It is for this reason that some companies include a note in their annual reports giving the market value of their shares at that date. (British Vita does not do so because it was not then a listed company.)

CLOSE COMPANIES

The Finance Act 1965 introduced the concept of the 'close company', defined as a company resident in the United Kingdom which is under the control of five or fewer participators and associates or of participators who are directors. The detailed legislation is extremely complex but has been of little practical importance since 1980. British Vita states in its directors' report that it is not a close company (Appendix C, p. 12).

TAX LAW

The most important statutes (Acts of Parliament) relating to the taxes described in this chapter are the Finance Acts 1965 and 1972, the Capital Allowances Act 1968, the Income and Corporation Taxes Act

1970 and the Taxes Management Act 1970. Every year there is at least one Finance Act amending the law. There is also a large body of case law relating to taxation. The law is thus always changing and some of the statements made in this chapter will need modification as the years go by.

AUDIT

The preparation of the financial statements of a company and their presentation to the shareholders and to the tax authorities are the duties of the directors, not of the auditors, although the latter, of course, often give valuable assistance. Since there are often misconceptions about the functions of auditors, it is worth looking carefully at the report they give.

The Report of the Auditors to the members (i.e. shareholders) of British Vita Company Ltd (Appendix C, p. 14) reads as follows:

We have examined the accounts set out on pages 15 to 25 and 28. Incorporated in these accounts are accounts of overseas subsidiaries and overseas associated companies audited by other firms who have reported thereon directly to us.

In our opinion the accounts which have been prepared on the historical cost basis of accounting modified for revaluation of certain fixed assets give, so far as concerns members of the Company, a true and fair view of the state of affairs at 31 December 1979 and of the profit and source and application of funds for the year ended on that date and comply with the Companies Acts 1948 and 1967.

We have also examined the current cost accounts set out on pages 26 and 27. In our opinion they have been prepared in accordance with the bases included in the notes to those accounts.

There are a number of interesting points to note about this report:

1. it is a report, not a certificate or guarantee: the auditors report their opinion, they do not certify or guarantee anything;

2. what they give their opinion on is the 'truth and fairness' of the accounts. This is not the same as saying that the accounts are 'correct' in every particular. It should be clear from the discussion of the financial statements in chapter 2 that the figures in balance sheets and profit and loss accounts are necessarily based to a certain extent on judgments;

3. the auditors are reporting to the members (shareholders) of British Vita, not to the directors. Their function, as a late nineteenth-century English judge put it, is to serve as a 'watchdog' for the shareholders. They are appointed by the shareholders, usually on the recommendation of the directors. Appointment is made each year by resolution at the annual general meeting;

4. no reference is made to the discovery of mistakes or fraud. These are regarded as incidental to the main purpose of reporting as to 'truth and fairness';

5. the source and application of funds statement (required by an accounting standard but not by law) has been audited but the statement of value added required neither by law nor by an accounting standard has not been audited.

It is obviously important that auditors should not only be skilled in their profession but also be independent of the directors and managers of the company being audited. It is therefore provided by the Companies Acts that (1) auditors should either be members of a body of accountants established in the United Kingdom and recognized by the Department of Trade or be authorized by the Department to be appointed, and that (2) the auditor must not be an officer or servant of the company or of any company in the group, or a partner or employee of such officer or servant.

The amount of the auditors' remuneration must be stated in the annual report. For the British Vita group in 1979 it was £90,000, some of which was payable to auditors overseas (Appendix C, p. 18, note 2).

The references in the audit report to the historical cost basis and to the current cost accounts are explained in chapter 4.

4. Accounting Standards and Inflation

In order to draw up a set of financial statements for a company it is necessary to make decisions about:

1. what should be disclosed (*disclosure*);
2. the format of the statements (*presentation*);
3. the rules of measurement and valuation (*valuation*).

Who should make these decisions? There are a number of possibilities:

1. each company is allowed to decide for itself;
2. the accountancy profession, as acknowledged experts in the field, makes the decisions;
3. the government makes the decisions by means of
   (i) legislation,
   (ii) a government-controlled regulatory body,
   (iii) a national accounting plan, or
   (iv) an accounting court.

It is possible, of course, that a mixture of the above methods may be appropriate.

Whichever methods are chosen, there are costs and benefits. No one method is likely to be ideal for all countries and at all times. In this chapter we shall look at the British approach in the 1980s. It has to be remembered that it is the result of over a century of evolution and that British ideas on the subject are increasingly being influenced by the United States and the E.E.C. countries.

During the nineteenth century most British companies were allowed complete freedom in matters of disclosure, presentation and valuation. During the twentieth it gradually became accepted that, whilst the government should not interfere with presentation and valuation, it ought to prescribe by legislation what should be disclosed. This is the general philosophy behind the Companies Acts 1948 to 1980. The Acts impose two obligations on company directors: (1) to prepare balance sheets and profit and loss accounts which give a 'true and fair view', and (2) to give the detailed information specified in the Second Schedule to the 1967 Act. No definition is given of the phrase 'true and fair'.

This approach was commented on favourably in the report of the 1962 committee on company law amendment:

In our view the general scheme of the Act in this respect is the right one, namely to indicate in general terms the objectives and the standard of disclosure required and also to prescribe certain specific information that must be given. The formula 'true and fair' seems to us satisfactory as an indication of the required standard, while it makes for certainty to prescribe certain specific information which the law regards as the minimum necessary for the purpose of attaining that standard.*

The Committee went on to state that 'it is primarily to the initiative of the professional associations that we must look if the general principles of the Act are to be effectively applied in practice' (para. 334). They referred in particular to the Recommendations on Accounting Principles issued periodically by the Institute of Chartered Accountants in England and Wales (the 'English Institute'). It was through these Recommendations (issued between 1942 and 1969) that the professional accountancy bodies began to involve themselves in matters of presentation and valuation.

During the 1960s the quality of published financial statements was increasingly criticized. The profession responded in 1970 with the establishment of an Accounting Standards Committee (A.S.C.). It is known that the establishment of such a committee was encouraged by the government.

The British government has made no serious attempt to control company financial statements through a regulatory agency (as exists in the United States in the form of the Securities and Exchange Commission), a national accounting plan (as in France) or an accounting court (as in the Netherlands). It has, however, intervened on matters of disclosure and in the debate about inflation accounting (see

* *Report of the Company Law Committee* (Cmnd. 1749, 1962), para. 332.

below) and, as a result of Britain's entry into the E.E.C., it is legislating on presentation and valuation.

In Britain, then, it is company legislation and the accounting standards published by the A.S.C. which largely determine what goes into published financial statements. Less important influences are tax legislation and the requirements of the Stock Exchange. Tax legislation influences published accounts because companies may find it inconvenient to follow one set of practices for tax purposes and another for reporting to shareholders. Accounting practices banned for tax calculations tend to be unpopular in published financial statements, but there is no compulsion for a company to follow tax rules in those statements. (In this respect Britain differs from many continental European countries.)

Stock Exchange requirements for listed companies do not go much beyond those of company law and the accountancy profession. Listed companies are expected to comply with statements of standard accounting practice (see below).

The relevant requirements of the Companies Acts 1948 to 1980 are summarized in the Glossary (Appendix B) under a number of headings, the most important of which are: Balance Sheet, Directors' Emoluments, Directors' Report, Distributable Reserves, Fixed Assets, Group Accounts, Liabilities, Loans Receivable, Profit and Loss Account, Subsidiary, Turnover and Undistributable Reserves.

The E.E.C. Fourth Directive will be implemented through the Companies Act 1981. It will affect disclosure, presentation and valuation. Tables 1 and 2 illustrate the likely formats of balance sheets and profit and loss accounts.

The Accounting Standards Committee is composed of 23 part-time, unpaid accountants in private practice, industry or academic life. It is possible, but not certain, that it will be reconstituted to include users as well as preparers of financial statements. It operates by issuing 'exposure drafts' for comment by interested parties. Later, a definitive statement is issued and disclosure must be made (by the auditor if the company itself does not do so) of any departures therefrom in published financial statements. If the auditor does not believe the departure to be justified, he will qualify his report.

As at 30 September 1980, eighteen Statements of Standard Accounting Practice (SSAPs) had been issued:

TABLE 1: *Balance Sheet Format*

	£	£
Fixed assets		
Intangible assets		x
Tangible assets		x
Financial assets		x
		x
Current assets		
Stocks	x	
Debtors	x	
Investments	x	
Cash at bank and in hand	x	
	x	
Less:		
Creditors: Amounts becoming due and payable within one year	(x)	
Net current assets/liabilities		x
Total assets less current liabilities		x
Creditors: Amounts becoming due and payable after more than one year		(x)
Provisions for liabilities and charges		(x)
		£xx
Capital and reserves		
Subscribed capital called up		x
Share premium account		x
Revaluation reserve		x
Reserves		x
Profit (loss) brought forward	x	
Profit (loss) for the financial year	x	x
		£xx

(*Source: Company Accounting and Disclosure* (Cmnd. 7654, 1979), Part B, ch. III.)

1. accounting for the results of associated companies;
2. disclosure of accounting policies;
3. earnings per share;

TABLE 2: *Profit and Loss Account Format*

	£	£	
Turnover			xxx
Cost of sales			(xxx)
Gross profit/loss			xxx
Distribution costs			(xxx)
Administrative expenses			(xxx)
Other operating income			xxx
Operating profit/loss			xxx
Dividends from subsidiaries		x	
Dividends from participating interests		x	
		xx	
Interest on loans to group companies		x	
Interest on other loans		x	
		xx	
Other interest receivable		xx	xxx
Amounts written off investments			(xxx)
Interest payable to group companies	(x)		
Other interest payable	(x)		(xxx)
Profit/loss before tax			xxx
Corporation tax			(xxx)
Profit/loss after tax			xxx
Extraordinary income		x	
Less: tax thereon		(x)	xxx
Profit/loss for the year			£xxx

(*Source:* As for Table 1.)

4. the accounting treatment of government grants;

5. accounting for value added tax;

6. extraordinary items and prior year adjustments;

7. accounting for changes in the purchasing power of money (a provisional standard replaced by SSAP 16);

8. the treatment of taxation under the imputation system in the accounts of companies;

9. stocks and work in progress;
10. statements of source and application of funds;
11. accounting for deferred taxation (replaced by SSAP 15);
12. accounting for depreciation;
13. accounting for research and development;
14. group accounts;
15. accounting for deferred taxation;
16. current cost accounting;
17. accounting for post balance sheet events;
18. accounting for contingencies;

It will be noted that SSAPs 7 and 11 have already been replaced by new ones.

Statements of standard accounting practice are inevitably to some extent 'political' documents. The professional accountancy bodies have no legal right to lay down accounting practices or to say what must be disclosed in company financial statements. They do of course have authority over their own members. Where a company does not observe an accounting standard it is expected to disclose the fact and to explain its reasons. All significant departures from accounting standards will be referred to in the auditors' report, whether or not they are disclosed in the accounts. If the auditors consider that a departure is not justified they will qualify their report and, if practicable, they will also quantify the financial effect of the departure. In exceptional circumstances the directors may consider, and the auditors may agree, that a departure is required in order to show a true and fair view. In such a case, the auditors will mention it and their agreement to it but will not qualify their report.

Not all exposure drafts have become statements of standard accounting practice. That on acquisitions and mergers, for example, ran into considerable criticism and was never implemented.

The various statements of standard accounting practice are very important. References to them will be found throughout this book. The most general one is SSAP 2 on the disclosure of accounting policies. This sets out four basic assumptions or concepts which are said to underlie the periodic accounts of business enterprises:

(a) the 'going concern' concept: the enterprise will continue in operational existence for the foreseeable future;

(b) the 'accruals' concept: revenues and costs are accrued (i.e. recognised as they are earned or incurred, not as money is received or paid), matched with one another as far as their relationship can be established or justifiably assumed, and dealt with in the profit and loss account of the period to which they relate;

(c) the 'consistency' concept: there is consistency of accounting treatment of like items within each accounting period and from one period to the next;

(d) the 'prudence' concept: revenue and profits are not anticipated, but are recognised by inclusion in the profit and loss account only when realised in the form either of cash or of other assets the ultimate realisation of which can be assessed with reasonable certainty; provision is made for all known liabilities whether the amount of these is known with certainty or is a best estimate in the light of the information available.

Where there is a conflict between the accruals and prudence concepts the latter usually prevails.

Most accountants would agree that the above concepts are reasonably descriptive of actual practice; not all would accept that these are the concepts which *ought* to be followed. In particular there are those who think too much stress is laid on prudence, or conservatism as they would prefer to call it.

A concept not mentioned in SSAP 2 is 'objectivity'. Objectivity arises from the need to establish rules for recording financial transactions and events which as far as possible do not depend on the personal judgment of the recorder. This has led to a bias in favour of using the cost of acquisition, or historical cost as it is usually called. A brief description of traditional British accounting practice would be historical cost modified by prudence. Many accountants have denied that it is a function of a balance sheet to show how much a company is worth. It is, they have argued, merely a historical record. Other accountants have argued, however, that a balance sheet which did not attempt to show how much a company is worth would be of little use to the shareholders.

As a result of SSAP 2, companies publish statements of 'accounting policies' setting out the way in which they have dealt with a number of matters. British Vita's statement, for example (App. C, p. 15), covers the basis of consolidation, associated companies, deferred taxation, depreciation, stocks, grants, research and development, patents and trade marks, foreign currencies and comparative figures.

ACCOUNTING FOR INFLATION

In times of inflation, balance sheet values based on historical cost rapidly become divorced from current market values, and objectivity and prudence can lead paradoxically to an overstatement of profits. This is most easily understood in relation to fixed assets and depreciation. If fixed assets are valued at historical cost, depreciation will usually be based on historical cost as well. This will result in a lower depreciation charge, and hence a higher profit, than if both the asset and the depreciation were written up to, say, current replacement cost. It can be strongly argued that the use of historical costs during a period of inflation can lead to the publication of profit figures which are in part fictitious. The distribution of such profits would mean a running down of the *real* (as opposed to the money) capital of the company.

During the 1970s the rates of inflation experienced in Britain (see Table 3) were such that historical cost accounting came under increasing attack. The attempts by the leaders of the accountancy profession to introduce some form of inflation accounting were beset by many difficulties.*

TABLE 3: *Inflation Rates, 1971–9*

Year	Index (average for calendar year)	Percentage increase over the previous year %
1971	80·0	
1972	85·7	7·1
1973	93·5	9·1
1974	108·5	16·0
1975	134·8	24·2
1976	157·1	16·5
1977	182·0	15·8
1978	197·1	8·3
1979	223·5	13·4

(*Source:* Index of Retail Prices (1974 = 100) as reported in *Accountancy*.)

*For a lively account by a participant see C. A. Westwick, 'The Lessons to be Learned from the Development of Inflation Accounting in the U.K.', *Accounting and Business Research*, Autumn 1980.

Two principal methods of accounting for inflation were debated:

    1. adjustments for changes in the *general* price level only, i.e. current purchasing power (CPP) accounting;

    2. adjustments for changes in *specific* prices, i.e. current cost accounting (CCA).

No attempt will be made here to compare these methods. The A.S.C. originally preferred CPP accounting and this was the basis of the provisional SSAP 7 issued in 1974. The government-appointed Sandilands Committee, however, which reported in 1975, rejected CPP accounting in favour of CCA. The standard finally accepted in 1980, SSAP 16, is CCA based. SSAP 16 was preceded by an exposure draft (ED 24) and it is this which is referred to on page 26 of British Vita's 1979 Annual Report.

SSAP 16 applies to all listed companies and also to those companies which satisfy at least two of the following criteria:

    1. a turnover of £5 million p. a. or above;

    2. a balance sheet total in the historical cost accounts of £2·5 million or more; and

    3. an average number of employees in the U.K. of 250 or more.

These criteria are based on the E.E.C. Fourth Directive (see chapter 1) and may be amended to keep in line with company legislation.

SSAP 16 does not apply to certain specialized companies or to not-for-profit organizations.

Companies are given the option of presenting:

    1. historical cost accounts as the main accounts with supplementary current cost accounts;

    2. current cost accounts as the main accounts with supplementary historical cost accounts; or

    3. current cost accounts as the only accounts but accompanied by adequate historical cost information.

In its 1979 Annual Report (published before SSAP 16 came into force), British Vita chose the first of these.

In a current cost balance sheet assets are not valued at historical cost but at what is known as 'value to the business', i.e. the lower of net current replacement cost and 'recoverable amount' (the greater of net realizable value and the amount recoverable from further use). In practice this is likely to mean, as in the case of British Vita, that fixed assets are included at net current replacement cost and the stocks at the lower of *current replacement cost* and net realizable value (rather than the lower of *historical cost* and net realizable value).

Assets such as bank balances, debtors and creditors are valued as in the historical cost accounts. In principle, investments in associated companies should also be on a value to the business basis, but such information may be very difficult to obtain, especially if the associated companies are overseas. In 1979 British Vita continued to use historical cost as the information required to restate the figures was not readily available (App. C, p. 27, note 1(b)).

Liabilities are valued as in the historical cost accounts and no change is made to the share capital. A new reserve is introduced, called in ED 24 (and by British Vita) a 'capital maintenance reserve' and in SSAP 16 a 'current cost reserve'. Into this reserve is transferred an amount equal to all the adjustments necessary to convert historical cost accounts to current cost accounts. The current cost reserve represents the amount required by the group to maintain the operating capacity of its business, to the extent that this has not already been allowed for in the historical cost accounts.

In the profit and loss account four adjustments are made:

1. a cost of sales adjustment (COSA);
2. a monetary working capital adjustment (MWCA);
3. a depreciation adjustment; and
4. a gearing adjustment.

These adjustments are applied in two stages:

1. to arrive at a *current cost trading* (or operating) *profit*. Using British Vita's 1979 figures this is calculated as follows:

		£,000
Historical trading profit		6,875
Current cost adjustments:		
Cost of sales	(1,168)	
Monetary working capital	(467)	
Depreciation	(1,773)	
		(3,408)
Current cost trading profit		3,467

The current cost trading (operating) profit represents the surplus arising from the ordinary activities of the business, after allowing for the impact of price changes on the funds needed to continue the existing business and to maintain its operating capability, but without taking into account the way in which it is financed. It is calculated before interest and before taxation.

2. to arrive at the *current cost profit attributable to shareholders*. Using British Vita's 1979 figures this is calculated as follows:

	£000
Current cost trading profit	3,467
Share of profit of associated companies	3,129
Interest	(1,076)
Gearing adjustment	851
Profit before tax	6,371
Tax	(2,102)
Minority interest	(64)
Current cost profit attributable to shareholders	4,205

Current cost profit attributable to shareholders represents the surplus for the period after allowing for the impact of price changes on the funds needed to maintain the shareholders' proportion of the operating capabilities of the group.

Page 27 of British Vita's report gives more details of the adjustments. The cost of sales adjustment is made in order to base the cost of sales on the cost current at the time of consumption instead of the time of purchase. This can be done in various ways. British Vita has made use of appropriate price indices and has used the so-called averaging method, i.e. the adjustment is equal to the average *physical* stock multiplied by the price increase during the year.

Increased prices tie up in the business not only more stocks but also more monetary working capital (i.e., in essence, bank balances + debtors − creditors). The MWCA can be calculated by the averaging method in a similar way to the COSA. The depreciation adjustment is made in order to base depreciation on current replacement cost instead of historical cost.

The gearing adjustment is the most controversial. It is intended to indicate the benefit to shareholders of the use of long-term debt, measured by the extent to which the net operating assets are financed by borrowing. In effect, as calculated in SSAP 16, it reduces the three current cost adjustments by the proportion which has been financed by borrowing. The concept of 'gearing' is discussed further in chapter 8.

SSAP 16 does not solve all the problems of inflation accounting. For example, the 1980 statements will be in current 1980 figures, the 1981 statements in current 1981 figures. How can they be properly compared? One approach is to calculate ratios (see chapter 5) on each year's figures and to compare these instead.

Inflation accounting is still in its infancy and is by no means easy to understand. It is clear, however, that traditional historical cost accounting is no longer adequate and that SSAP 16 is likely to produce more relevant information to users of financial statements.

5. Tools of Analysis and Sources of Information

... high Heaven rejects the lore
Of nicely-calculated less or more

WILLIAM WORDSWORTH, *Inside of King's College Chapel, Cambridge*

The first four chapters of this book have been mainly descriptive. In the chapters which follow we turn to analysis and interpretation. We shall be concerned with three main questions:

1. is the company under analysis making a satisfactory profit?
2. is the company likely to run out of cash, or to keep cash idle?
3. how does the company decide the sources of its long-term funds?

These are the related problems of profitability, liquidity and capital structure.

Our tools of analysis will be the relationships which exist among the different items in the financial statements ('financial ratios') and the rates of return linking outflows with expected inflows ('yields').

FINANCIAL RATIOS

Financial ratios are normally expressed either as percentages or by the number of times one figure can be divided into another. For example, if a company has current assets of £10,000 and current liabilities of £5,000, we could say that current liabilities are 50 per cent of current assets, that current assets are 200 per cent of current liabilities, that the ratio $\frac{\text{current assets}}{\text{current liabilities}}$ is 2·0, or that the ratio $\frac{\text{current liabilities}}{\text{current assets}}$ is 0·5. Which method is chosen is a matter of convenience and convention. In the example quoted it is customary to speak of a current ratio, $\frac{\text{current assets}}{\text{current liabilities}}$, of 2·0.

A percentage, as can be seen from the above, is merely a ratio multiplied by 100.

Not all ratios and percentages are significant or useful and one must beware of the temptation to calculate them for their own sake. It is unlikely, for example, that much can be gained from a scrutiny of the relationship between current liabilities and goodwill. The limitations of conventional accounting must always be kept in mind and accounting figures should not be treated as more precise than they really are. There is little sense in calculating a ratio to more than two decimal places.

YIELDS

A yield is a rate of return relating outflows to inflows. If, for example, I buy for £50 an irredeemable government bond with a par value of £100 on which interest of 4 per cent is payable annually, there is an immediate cash outflow of £50, followed by a series of cash inflows of £4 each year in perpetuity. The yield (gross of tax) is $\frac{4 \times 100}{50}$%, i.e. 8%. If the bond were redeemable at a fixed price at some date in the future there would be a difference between the flat yield, which takes only the interest into account, and the redemption yield, which takes the redemption price into account as well. For example, if the bond is redeemable twenty years hence at par, the flat yield is about 5·0 per cent and the redemption yield about 9·8 per cent. Yields such as these can be calculated using compound interest tables, specially compiled bond tables or a suitable computer program.

THE NEED FOR COMPARISONS

Any ratio, percentage or yield is of little value in isolation. It is necessary to have some standard with which to compare it. The standard can be a budgeted one, set by the company for itself; a historical one, based on the past performance of the company; or an industry one, based on the observed ratios of companies in the same industry.

Budgeted standards are not usually available to shareholders or external financial analysts. Historical comparisons are often given in annual reports: see, for example, page 13 of British Vita's report, headed 'British Vita Group 1975–1979'.

INDUSTRY RATIOS

Industry ratios pose a much more difficult problem to the financial analyst. There are a number of reasons for this.

First, it is often difficult to decide to which industry a company belongs. Many industries are, in fact, composed of a surprisingly heterogeneous group of companies. In the Stock Exchange industrial classification British Vita is included in the plastics and rubber fabricators group, which is only a partial indication of the range of the group's activities. Extel Statistical Services Ltd includes British Vita under the following industry headings: motor vehicle components; weaving of cotton, linen and man-made fibres; textile finishing; footwear; other rubber goods; plastics products not elsewhere specified; and road haulage contracting for general hire or reward.

Secondly, the emphasis of the system of accounting at present in use is on *consistency* for a particular company over time, rather than *comparability* among different companies at a single point in time, and the analyst must constantly be on his guard against differences in definition and in methods of valuation.

For these reasons not too much reliance can be placed on an industry comparison which is based on ratios obtained from published accounts. Companies can, however, obtain comparable ratios by taking part in a properly conducted comparison, such as those conducted by the Centre for Interfirm Comparison.* Such ratios are, however, by their very nature, confidential and unavailable to the external analyst.

SOURCES OF INFORMATION

In this section are listed a number of useful sources of information relating to individual companies, to industries or to the company sector as a whole. The list is not intended to be exhaustive. Most of the items should be available in a good public or university library. The Central Statistical Office publishes each year a brief, up-to-date guide

* See H. Ingham and L. T. Harrington, *Interfirm Comparison* (Heinemann, 1980).

to government statistics. There is also a more comprehensive *Guide to Official Statistics*.

1. *The Times 1000* (published annually by *The Times*)

This lists each year, amongst other things, the thousand largest British industrial companies, with details of their turnover (both total and export); capital employed (defined as total tangible assets less current liabilities and sundry provisions, other than bank loans and overdrafts and deferred tax); net profit before interest and tax; net profit before interest and tax as a percentage of turnover; net profit before interest and tax as a percentage of capital employed; number of employees; and the market capitalization of the equity (i.e. the total market value of all the company's ordinary shares). British Vita is one of the thousand.

2. *Company Finance* (available annually by subscription from H.M.S.O.; it is M3 in the 'Business Monitor' series)

Contains tables showing for both listed and non-listed companies, and by industrial sector:

   (i) a balance sheet summary;
  (ii) appropriation of trading and other income;
 (iii) sources and uses of funds;
 (iv) supplementary information (turnover, exports, political contributions, etc.);
  (v) various accounting ratios;
 (vi) size distributions.

3. *Financial Statistics* (published monthly by the Central Statistical Office; an 'explanatory handbook' is published annually)

Section 9 gives balance sheet, profit and loss account and funds statement data for industrial and commercial companies as a whole. More up-to-date than *Company Finance*.

4. *British Business* (published weekly by the Departments of Industry and Trade)

5. *Economic Trends* (published monthly by H.M.S.O.)

6. *Bank of England Quarterly Bulletin*

7. *National Income and Expenditure* (the 'Blue Book'; published annually by H.M.S.O.)

Statistics on the company sector are published from time to time in numbers 4 to 7. The first three also carry useful articles interpreting the statistics.

8. *Extel Cards* (Extel Statistical Services Ltd, London)

The cards provide information (kept continually up to date) based on the financial statements and stock market performance of individual companies.

9. *The Stock Exchange Fact Book* (published quarterly by the Stock Exchange)

A wealth of information on all aspects of the British stock market.

10. *The Stock Exchange Official Year-Book* (published annually by the Stock Exchange)

11. *Survey of Published Accounts* (published annually by the Institute of Chartered Accountants in England and Wales)

A guide to current accounting requirements and an analysis of methods and examples of financial reporting used by 300 major British industrial companies and by major property companies and investment trusts.

12. *Accounting Standards* (published annually by the Institute of Chartered Accountants in England and Wales)

Contains the full texts of all U.K. exposure drafts and accounting standards extant at 1 May each year. Also contains background material on the Accounting Standards Committee.

13. *Current Accounting Law and Practice* (published annually by Sweet & Maxwell)

Reproduces all relevant statute law, case law and accounting standards.

14. *Price Index Numbers for Current Cost Accounting* (published monthly by the Department of Industry)

Essential data for the preparation of current cost accounts.

15. *Sources of British Business Comparative Performance Data* (no. 96 in the Accountants Digest Series published by the Institute of Chartered Accountants in England and Wales)

6. Profitability and Return on Investment

For what is Worth in anything
But so much Money as 'twill bring
SAMUEL BUTLER, *Hudibras*, I., i.

PROFITABILITY

One of the first questions a shareholder is likely to ask of his company is: is it making a profit? If so, is it making a satisfactory profit? In this chapter we shall look at the British Vita group's profit record for the four years 1976–9. Most of the figures we shall need are given on p. 13 of the 1979 annual report.

RETURN ON INVESTMENT

Sales and profits should not be looked at in isolation from the investment made to achieve them.

Return on investment may be defined as

$$\frac{\text{profit}}{\text{assets}} \times 100\%$$

Both 'profit' and 'assets' have a number of possible meanings. They can be measured in either historical cost or current cost terms. It is usual in this context to take a profit figure before interest and tax in order to separate managerial performance from the effects of different financial structures (see chapter 8) and from changes in tax rates. Exceptional, extraordinary and prior year items are also excluded. Assets must be defined consistently to be net of current liabilities but not of what British Vita calls external sources (loans, long-term creditors and minority interests). Assets so defined are equal in amount to shareholders' funds plus external sources ('capital employed' in British Vita's terminology).

On page 13 of its 1979 annual report British Vita calculates profit before tax and interest as a percentage of *average* capital employed. The details of the calculations are given in Table 4. It will be noted that

TABLE 4: *Calculation of Historical Cost Return on Investment, British Vita Company Ltd, 1976–9*

	Trading profit (a) £,ooo	Share of profit of associated companies (b) £,ooo	Profit before interest and tax (c) = (a) + (b) £,ooo	Capital employed (d) £,ooo	Average capital employed (e)* £,ooo	Profit before tax and interest as a percentage of average capital employed (f) = (c)/(e) × 100 %
1976	1,409	3,084	4,493	15,679	14,078	31·9
1977	3,122	3,561	6,683	20,646	18,162	36·8
1978	4,482	2,793	7,275	24,914	22,780	31·9
1979	6,875	3,129	10,004	32,734	28,824	34·7

* Average capital employed for 1979 is equal to the average of capital employed 1978 and capital employed 1979, and similarly for other years.

(*Source*: British Vita Company Ltd, Annual Report and Accounts 1979, page 13.)

profit before tax and interest is equal to trading profit *plus* share of profit of associated companies.

RELATIONSHIP OF PROFIT TO TURNOVER

It is often considered helpful to analyse the return on investment ratio as follows:

$$\frac{\text{profit}}{\text{assets}} = \frac{\text{profit}}{\text{sales}} \times \frac{\text{sales}}{\text{assets}}$$

Unfortunately it is difficult to do this when the share of profits of associated companies is a material item, as is the case with the British Vita group. It is difficult because although profit before interest and tax includes the share of profits of associated companies, sales (turnover), as we have seen, does *not* include a share of the turnover of the associated companies. It is for this reason that British Vita compares its turnover with trading profit, not with profit before interest and tax. The calculations are given in Table 5.

Table 4 shows that in historical cost terms the group more than doubled both profit before interest and tax and average capital employed during the period 1976–9. The return on investment was relatively stable. An interesting feature is the declining share of profit contributed by the associated companies. Table 5 shows a steadily increasing trading profit as a percentage of turnover.

TABLE 5: *Calculation of Historical Cost Trading Profit as Percentage of Turnover, British Vita Company Ltd, 1976–9*

	Turnover	Trading profit	Trading profit as a percentage of turnover
	(a)	(b)	(c) = (b)/(a) × 100
	£000	£000	%
1976	37,907	1,409	3·7
1977	44,042	3,122	7·1
1978	49,874	4,482	9·0
1979	73,296	6,875	9·4

(*Source:* British Vita Company Ltd, Annual Report and Accounts 1979, page 13.)

TABLE 6: *Comparison of Historical Cost Profitability Ratios*

	Profit before tax and interest as a percentage of average capital employed			Trading profit as a percentage of turnover		
	British Vita group	Manufacturing and distribution companies (listed)	Manufacturing and distribution companies (unlisted)	British Vita group	Manufacturing and distribution companies (listed)	Manufacturing and distribution companies (unlisted)
	%	%	%	%	%	%
1976	32	18	19	4	6	4
1977	37	18	22	7	6	6

Note: Trading profit is net of depreciation and hire of plant and machinery.
(*Sources:* 1. As for Tables 1 and 2.   2. *Company Finance* (H.M.S.O.), Eleventh Issue, 1980, tables 2, 4, 11 and 12.)

Current cost information has not been available until recently and, although British Vita has provided a current cost profit and loss account for a number of years, the measurement of current cost trading profit has varied from year to year in accordance with changes in proposed standard accounting practice. From 1979 onwards, however, consistent current cost information should be available.

In 1979, British Vita's current cost trading profit was £3,467,000 as compared with a historical cost trading profit of £6,875,000 (see App. C, p. 27). Current cost trading profit as a percentage of turnover was 4·7 per cent, just half the historical cost percentage of 9·4.

COMPARISONS

Table 6 provides a comparison of British Vita's historical cost profitability ratios with those of listed and non-listed British manufacturing and distribution companies for the years 1976 and 1977. It will be noted that British Vita is a relatively profitable group and that non-listed manufacturing and distributing companies appear to be more profitable than listed.

WAGES, TURNOVER AND VALUE ADDED

Trading profit as a percentage of turnover is a residual of a number of items whose relationship to turnover is also of interest. Unfortunately little information is usually available about these items. The ratio of British Vita's personnel charges to both turnover and value added can, however, be calculated from the group's statements of value added.

Table 7 shows for 1977–9 the total wages, salaries, pension and social security contributions for each year; the percentage increase or decrease on the previous year; wages, etc. as a percentage of turnover; and wages, etc. as a percentage of value added.

Personnel charges increased by 15 per cent in 1978 and by no less than 43 per cent in 1979 but remained a constant 23 per cent of turnover. In both 1977 and 1978, 59 per cent of value added was applied to personnel charges but this fell to 56 per cent in 1979. The main reason for the fall was an increase in dividends, which had been held back by government restriction in previous years (see chapter 8).

TABLE 7: *British Vita Company Ltd: Personnel Charges, Turnover and Value Added, 1977–9*

	Wages, salaries, pension and social security contributions	Percentage increase or decrease on previous year	As percentage of turnover	As percentage of value added
	£,000	%	%	%
1977	10,153		23	59
1978	11,632	+15	23	59
1979	16,662	+43	23	56

Note: Turnover excludes taxes.
Source: British Vita Company Ltd, Annual Reports and Accounts 1977, 1978 and 1979: Statements of Added Value.)

7. Liquidity and Cash Flows

One may not doubt that, somehow, good
Shall come of water and of mud;
And, sure, the reverent eye must see
A purpose in liquidity

RUPERT BROOKE, *Heaven*

LIQUIDITY

It is very important that a company should be profitable; it is just as important that it should be liquid. We have already seen (pp. 21–3) that an increase in profits must by definition lead to an increase in a company's net assets. There is no reason, however, why its *liquid* assets, such as cash in the bank, should automatically increase. A profitable and fast-expanding company may in fact find that it has tied up so much of its profits in fixed assets, stocks and debtors that it has difficulty in paying its debts as they fall due. To help prevent such a situation developing a company should prepare a cash budget, i.e. a plan of future cash receipts and payments based on specified assumptions about such things as sales growth, credit terms, issues of shares and expansion of plant. A simplified example demonstrating how a profitable company may run into liquidity problems is given below.

Oodnadatta Ltd is formed on 1 January 1982 to make boomerangs at a cost of £1.50 each and to sell them for £2 each. All bills are paid immediately and debts are collected within thirty days. The stock of boomerangs manufactured and paid for in January, for example, will be sold in February and the cash proceeds collected in March. The company's provisional plans are to sell 400 boomerangs in February 1982, 600 in March, 800 in April and so on. At 1 January the company has £600 in cash (raised by an issue of shares) – i.e. just sufficient to cover the manufacture of the first 400 boomerangs – but no other assets.

Before actually starting production the company draws up the following monthly budgets relating to profits and cash resources (Table 8).

The figures show that although the planned profit for the year

TABLE 8: *Oodnadatta Ltd: Cash Budget and Budgeted Profit and Loss Statement, 1982*

Budgeted Profit and Loss Statement

	Jan. £	Feb. £	Mar. £	Apr. £	May £	June £	July £	Aug. £	Sep. £	Oct. £	Nov. £	Dec. £	Total £
Sales	—	800	1,200	1,600	2,000	2,400	2,800	3,200	3,600	4,000	4,400	4,800	30,800
Cost of sales	—	600	900	1,200	1,500	1,800	2,100	2,400	2,700	3,000	3,300	3,600	23,100
Profit	—	200	300	400	500	600	700	800	900	1,000	1,100	1,200	7,700

Note: The sales figures are equal to the quantity sold multiplied by £2; the cost of sales figures to the quantity sold multiplied by £1·50; the profit figures to the quantity sold multiplied by £0·50. Note that the cost of sales figures give the cost of the goods *sold* during the month *not* the cost of the goods *manufactured* during the month.

Cash Budget

	Jan. £	Feb. £	Mar. £	Apr. £	May £	June £	July £	Aug. £	Sep. £	Oct. £	Nov. £	Dec. £
Balance at beginning of month	+600	—	—900	—1,300	—1,600	—1,800	—1,900	—1,900	—1,800	—1,600	—1,300	—900
Cash received from debtors	—	—	+800	+1,200	+1,600	+2,000	+2,400	+2,800	+3,200	+3,600	+4,000	+4,400
	+600	—	—100	—100	—	+200	+500	+900	+1,400	+2,000	+2,700	+3,500
Cash payments to creditors	—600	—900	—1,200	—1,500	—1,800	—2,100	—2,400	—2,700	—3,000	—3,300	—3,600	—3,900
Balance at end of month	—	—900	—1,300	—1,600	—1,800	—1,900	—1,900	—1,800	—1,600	—1,300	—900	—400

Note: Cash received from debtors is equal to the sales of the previous month; cash payments to creditors to the cost of sales of the next month.

is £7,700, cash will fall by £1,000 from a positive £600 to a negative £400. There is thus £8,700 to be accounted for. We can see what will happen by comparing the balance sheet at 1 January with that which will result at 31 December (Table 9).

TABLE 9: *Oodnadatta Ltd: Balance Sheets, 1 January & 31 December 1982*

Balance Sheets	1 Jan. 1982	31 Dec. 1982	Difference
	£	£	£
Cash	+600	−400	−1,000
Debtors	—	+4,800	+4,800
Stocks	—	+3,900	+3,900
	+600	+8,300	+7,700
Share capital	+600	+600	—
Retained profits	—	+7,700	+7,700
	+600	+8,300	+7,700

Note: The cash figure at 31 December is taken from the cash budget; the debtors represent the December sales, the cash for which will not be collected until January; the stocks represent the cost of goods manufactured and paid for in December for sale in January 1983.

The difference column, which is in fact a simple funds statement, shows the position quite clearly. All the profits, plus the original cash (£600), plus another £400 are tied up in debtors and stocks. It is interesting to note, however, that by the end of January 1983 the company's liquidity crisis will be over:

	Jan. 1983
Balance at beginning of month	−400
Cash received from debtors	+4,800
	+4,400
Cash payments to creditors	−4,200
	£ +200

The catch is, of course, that in its present under-capitalized state the company will never reach January 1983, in spite of its excellent profit-making potential, unless it can raise more cash by borrowing, by collecting its debts faster or by keeping down the size of its stocks.

If sales continue to rise similarly in 1983 and costs also remain the same, the company will run into the opposite problem: excess liquidity. The purpose of drawing up cash budgets is to ensure that the company neither runs out of cash nor keeps cash idle when it could be profitably invested.

CURRENT AND QUICK RATIOS

Although cash budgets are thus an essential part of internal company financial management, they are unavailable to the external financial analyst who must therefore use rather less precise measures of liquidity. What he tries to do is to approximate the possible future cash flows as closely as possible. It will be remembered that current assets and current liabilities were defined in chapter 2 as those assets and liabilities which can reasonably be expected to take the form of cash within one year from the date of the balance sheet. One crude measure of liquidity, therefore, is the relationship between the current assets and current liabilities. This is known as the 'current ratio', and is defined as follows:

$$\text{current ratio} = \frac{\text{current assets}}{\text{current liabilities}}$$

A more immediate measure of liquidity can be found by excluding stocks from the numerator. The resulting ratio is known as the quick, liquid or acid-test ratio:

$$\text{quick ratio} = \frac{\text{current assets} - \text{stocks}}{\text{current liabilities}}$$

It has the incidental advantage of being more easily compared among companies, since it does not depend, as does the current ratio to some extent, on the method chosen to value the stock-in-trade.

The current assets, stocks and current liabilities of the British Vita group at the end of its 1976, 1977, 1978 and 1979 financial years can easily be extracted from its 1977, 1978 and 1979 group balance sheets (the first two are not reprinted in this book).

In Table 10 (p. 76) the current and quick ratios have been calculated.

Tables 11 and 12 compare the current and quick ratios of the British Vita group and of listed and unlisted manufacturing and distribution companies in general for the years 1976 and 1977 (figures were not available for 1978 and 1979 at the time of writing).

TABLE 10: *British Vita Company Ltd: Calculation of Current and Quick Ratios, 1976–9*

	Current assets	Stocks	Current assets less Stocks	Current liabilities	Current ratio	Quick ratio
	(a)	(b)	(c) = (a) − (b)	(d)	(a)/(d)	(c)/(d)
	£000	£000	£000	£000		
1976	15,342	5,135	10,207	11,682	1·31	0·87
1977	18,003	5,521	12,482	13,421	1·34	0·93
1978	22,201	7,211	14,990	16,507	1·34	0·91
1979	32,507	10,190	22,317	26,128	1·24	0·85

(*Source:* British Vita Company Ltd, Annual Reports and Accounts 1977, 1978 and 1979.)

TABLE 11: *Comparison of Current Ratios*

	British Vita group	Manufacturing and distribution companies Listed	Unlisted
1976	1·31	1·53	1·38
1977	1·34	1·56	1·44

(*Sources:* 1. British Vita Company Ltd, Annual Reports and Accounts 1977 and 1978. *Company Finance* (H.M.S.O.), Eleventh Issue, 1980, tables 2 and 4.)

TABLE 12: *Comparison of Quick Ratios*

	British Vita group	Manufacturing and distribution companies Listed	Unlisted
1976	0·87	0·84	0·74
1977	0·93	0·85	0·76

(*Sources:* As for Table 11.)

It can be seen that British Vita's liquidity has changed little over the three years. On a comparison of current ratios the group is less liquid than companies in general; on a quick ratio basis it is more liquid. Unlisted companies tend to be less liquid than listed companies.

DEFENSIVE INTERVAL

Both the current ratio and the quick ratio are static rather than dynamic, i.e. they treat liquidity as something to be measured at a point in time rather than over a period. A more dynamic approach would be to divide the quick assets not by the current liabilities but by those operating expenses which require the use of quick assets, i.e. in terms of the information available in British Vita's statement of value added, the bought-in materials and services, the wages and salaries, etc., taxes and interest on loans (but not the dividends if the analysis is from the point of view of the shareholders). Depreciation is not included as it is not a cash expense. The calculations for British Vita are shown in Table 13. The result of the calculation, measured in days by multiplying the ratio by 365, can be called the 'defensive interval'. It would be preferable to use forecast rather than past operating expenses, but these, of course, are not available to the external analyst.

TABLE 13: *British Vita Company Ltd: Calculation of Defensive Intervals, 1976–9*

	Quick Assets (= col. c of Table 10) (a)	Operating Expenses requiring use of Quick Assets (b)	Defensive Interval (days) (c) = (a)/(b) × 365
1976	10,207	40,761	91
1977	12,482	45,255	101
1978	14,990	50,132	109
1979	22,317	73,953	110

(*Source:* British Vita Company Ltd, Annual Reports and Accounts.)

Once again the ratio indicates little change in recent years in British Vita's liquidity.

AVERAGE COLLECTION PERIOD AND STOCK TURNOVER

Another important indicator of liquidity is the speed at which debts are collected. The average collection period for debtors can be calculated as follows, if one assumes that all sales are for credit:

$$\frac{\text{average debtors} \times 365}{\text{sales}} \text{ days}$$

Average debtors are defined as the mean of the opening and closing debtors figures. It is preferable to use averages when, as in the case of British Vita, the size of the figures differs considerably from year to year.

Another way of looking at the average collection period would be to think in terms of debtors turnover: $\frac{\text{sales}}{\text{average debtors}}$. The relationship between stock and sales is usually looked at in this way: stock turnover $= \frac{\text{sales}}{\text{average stock}}$. In assessing these ratios it must be remembered that they are weighted averages. There may be important differences per product and per geographical area which only more detailed accounts would reveal.

Table 14 shows how British Vita's average collection period and stock turnover can be calculated.

TABLE 14: *British Vita Company Ltd: Calculation of Average Collection Period and Stock Turnover, 1977–9*

	Sales	Average Debtors	Average Stocks	Average Collection Period	Stock Turnover
	(a)	(b)	(c)	(b)/(a) × 365 days	(a)/(c)
	£000	£000	£000		
1977	44,042	10,332	5,328	86	8·27
1978	49,874	12,103	6,366	89	7·83
1979	73,296	16,789	8,700	84	8·42

(*Source:* British Vita Company Ltd, Annual Reports and Accounts 1977, 1978 and 1979.)

Once again the ratios are shown to be fairly stable over time.

PREDICTING INSOLVENCY

The extreme case of illiquidity is insolvency, which occurs when a company is unable to pay its debts as they fall due.

Is it possible to use financial ratios to predict insolvency in advance?

Researchers in both the U.S.A. and the U.K. have approached this problem by examining the ratios of companies just prior to their insolvency. It is possible by the use of statistical techniques to calculate a 'score' for companies based on a number of relevant ratios appropriately weighted. Companies with scores over a certain range are more likely to become insolvent.

As is usual in ratio analysis, it is necessary to use more than one ratio and the result is a guide, not a certainty. A company with a bad score is not certain to become insolvent, but only more likely to.

WINDOW-DRESSING

We will end this chapter with an illustration of a problem which arises from the nature of ratios. Suppose that a company has current assets of £800,000, current liabilities of £500,000 and quick assets of £550,000. Its *net* current assets and *net* quick assets will therefore be £300,000 and £50,000 respectively. If we keep these *net* amounts constant but vary the gross figures using current assets to pay off current liabilities, then the current and quick ratios will vary as shown in Table 15.

TABLE 15: *Illustration of Window-Dressing*

Current assets (*a*) £000	*Current liabilities* (*b*) £000	*Quick assets* (*c*) £000	*Current ratio* (*a*)/(*b*)	*Quick ratio* (*c*)/(*b*)
800	500	550	1·60	1·10
700	400	450	1·75	1·12
600	300	350	2·00	1·17
500	200	250	2·50	1·25
400	100	150	4·00	1·50
350	50	100	7·00	2·00
301	1	51	301·00	51·00

Obviously we have exaggerated to make a point, but there is clearly some latitude for window-dressing. Within limits, a company may be able to arrange its current assets and liabilities so as to have the desired ratios at balance-sheet time.

8. Sources of Funds and Capital Structure

Les affaires, c'est bien simple: c'est l'argent des autres

ALEXANDRE DUMAS, fils, *La question d'argent*

SOURCES OF FUNDS

The funds available to a company are obtained either from its share-holders or by borrowing. The former includes not only issues of shares but also the retention of profits. The latter range from long-term debt to trade credit. The composition at any time of these sources, and more especially the long-term sources, is referred to as the 'capital structure' of a company. Table 16 gives some ideas of the relative importance of various sources for listed manufacturing and distribution companies in the years 1976 and 1977. Figures for British Vita in 1977, 1978 and 1979 are given in Table 17.

Four points in particular stand out from Table 16:

1. by far the most important source of funds is the ordinary shareholders, especially through the medium of reserves (which consist mainly of retained profits);

2. preference shares are of very minor importance;

3. deferred taxation is an important but rather ambiguous item: is it equity or debt or both?

4. long-term loans are important although well behind reserves.

Table 17 shows the importance of ordinary shareholders' funds to the British Vita group, but also that the expansion of 1978 and 1979 owed much to an increase in the relative importance of long-term loans in the group's capital structure. Ordinary shareholders' funds made up 82·0 per cent of long-term finance in 1977, 78·4 per cent in 1978 and 74·5 per cent in 1979.

Using current cost instead of historical cost data the 1979 figures would have been as shown on page 82.

TABLE 16: *Sources of Funds, U.K. Listed Manufacturing and Distribution Companies, 1976, 1977 and 1978*

	1976		1977	
	£m.	%	£m.	%
Ordinary shares	8,288	18	8,719	17
Reserves	21,949	47	26,948	52
Ordinary shareholders' funds	30,237	65	35,667	68
Preference shares	450	1	515	1
Deferred taxation	6,271	13	5,522	11
Minority interests	1,870	4	1,877	4
Long-term loans	7,997	17	8,552	16
	46,825	100	52,133	100
Bank overdrafts and loans	9,159		10,099	

(*Source:* Calculated from figures given in *Company Finance* (H.M.S.O.), Eleventh Issue, 1980, table 2.)

TABLE 17: *Sources of Funds, British Vita Group, 1977, 1978 and 1979*

	1977		1978		1979	
	£000	%	£000	%	£000	%
Ordinary shares	3,407	16·5	4,118	16·5	4,971	15·2
Reserves	13,518	65·5	15,416	61·9	19,430	59·4
Ordinary share-holders' funds	16,925	82·0	19,534	78·4	24,401	74·5
Preference shares	57	0·3	57	0·2	57	0·2
Deferred taxation	—		—		—	
Minority interests	—	—	102	0·4	265	0·8
Long-term loans and creditors	3,664	17·7	5,221	21·0	8,011	24·5
	20,646	100·0	24,914	100·0	32,734	100·0
Bank overdrafts	595		927		3,263	

(*Source:* British Vita Company Ltd, Annual Reports and Accounts 1978 and 1979.)

	£000	%
Ordinary shares	4,971	11·7
Reserves	29,026	68·6
Ordinary shareholders' funds	33,997	80·3
Preference shares	57	0·2
Minority interests	265	0·6
Long-term loans and creditors	8,011	18·9
	42,330	100·00

The reserves are larger because of the effect of writing up assets to current replacement costs. It is clear that the use of historical cost data may understate the importance of shareholders' funds.

CAPITAL STRUCTURE

Is there such a thing as an optimal capital structure for a particular company? This is a question which has aroused much academic debate. In principle there probably is such a structure, but it is not easy in practice for a company either to discover what it is or to achieve it.

The main problem is to choose the best mix of debt (loans, debentures) and equity (ordinary shares, reserves, retained profits). There is no easy way of doing this. It is possible to list the factors which ought to be considered, but assessing the weight to be given to each remains very largely a matter of judgment and experience. The factors are:

1. *Cost:* The current and future costs of each potential source of capital should be estimated and compared. It should be borne in mind that the costs of each source are not necessarily independent of each other. An increase in debt now, for example, may push up the cost of equity later. Other things being equal, it is desirable to minimize the average overall cost of capital to the company.

2. *Risk:* It is unwise (and often disastrous) to place a company in a position where it may be unable, if profits fall even temporarily, to pay interest as it falls due or to meet redemptions. It is equally undesirable to be forced to cut or omit the ordinary dividend (see the section below on dividend policy).

3. *Control:* Except where there is no alternative, a company should not make any issue of shares which will have the effect of removing or diluting control by the existing shareholders.

4. *Acceptability:* A company can only borrow if others are willing to lend to it. Few listed companies can afford the luxury of a capital structure which is unacceptable to financial institutions. A company with readily mortgageable assets will find it easier to raise debt.

5. *Transferability:* Shares may be listed or unlisted. Many private companies have made issues of shares to the public in order to obtain a stock exchange listing and to improve the transferability of their shares. Such a procedure may also have tax advantages.

Cost of capital and risk are discussed in more detail in the next two sections.

COST OF CAPITAL

Although a company cannot always choose what appears to be the cheapest source of capital, because of the need to pay attention to risk, control, acceptability and transferability, it should always estimate the cost of each potential source and the effect on the overall average cost.

A rather over-simplified approach is to work out first of all the cost of each potential source of capital. This is most easily done in the case of debentures. Suppose that a company can issue £100,000 10 per cent debentures at par, repayable at par in twenty years' time. The before-tax cost is obviously 10 per cent; the after-tax cost, assuming immediate payment and a corporation tax rate of 50 per cent, is 5 per cent. If preference shares were issued instead, the before- and after-tax rates would be equal, since preference dividends, unlike debenture interest, are not deductible for tax purposes. This explains why, since the introduction of corporation tax in 1965, many companies have replaced their preference share capital by loan stock. The introduction of the imputation system, however, has made preference shares a little more attractive.

The arithmetic becomes rather more difficult if the loan stock is not issued at par. In December 1970, for example, Imperial Chemical Industries Ltd made an issue of £40 million $10\frac{3}{4}$ per cent Unsecured

Loan Stock 1991/6 at £98 per cent, payable £20 per £100 stock on application, £40 on 1 March 1971 and £38 on 29 April 1971. That is, for every £98 received over the period December 1970 to April 1971 the company promised to pay interest of £10.75 each year and to repay the stock at par (£100) between 1991 and 1996. Using tables (or a computer program) it can be calculated that the yield to the last redemption date (1996) is a fraction under 11 per cent.

The real cost of issuing debentures is reduced during a period of inflation by the fact that the cash paid out by the company will be of lower purchasing power than the cash it receives at the date of issue.

Reckoning the cost of an issue of ordinary shares is more difficult. An analogous calculation to the one above would suggest that it is equal to the gross dividend yield, worked out as follows:

$$\frac{\text{current dividend per ordinary share} \times 100}{\text{market price per share}} \times \frac{10}{7}$$

The purpose of multiplying by 10/7 is to allow for the tax credit.

Dividend yields may be most easily found from the stock exchange pages of the *Financial Times* and other newspapers. The *F.T.* Share Information Service gives quite a lot of information about shares every day. The following typical entry has been extracted from the *Financial Times* of 20 August 1980 (referring to the day before):

1980 High	Low	Stock	Price	+ or −	Div. Net	Cover	Yield Gross	P/E
180	126	British Vita	149	+1	5·0	5·6	4·8	4·4

This tells us that the current market price of British Vita's ordinary shares (par value 25p) is 149p, compared with a high for the year of 180p, a low of 126p and a price the day before of 148p. (Par values may be assumed to be 25p unles the *F.T.* states otherwise.) The most recent dividend was 5·0p per share.

British Vita's dividend yield (gross) is calculated by the *F.T.* as follows:

$$\frac{\text{current dividend per ordinary share} \times 100}{\text{market price per share}} \times \frac{10}{7}$$

i.e.

$$\frac{5 \cdot 0 \times 100}{149} \times \frac{10}{7}\% = 4 \cdot 8\%$$

The dividend yield of any company can be compared with dividend yields in general and with those of other companies in the same equity group or sub-section, by looking at the table in the *Financial Times* headed 'F.T. – Actuaries Share Indices'. On 19 August 1980 the '500 Share' dividend yield was 6·46 per cent.

These yields can be contrasted with the 11·53 per cent yield on irredeemable government stocks and a redemption yield of 13·65 per cent on fifteen twenty-year redeemable debentures and loans. Given the relative riskiness of fixed-interest and variable-dividend securities this is at first sight surprising. Before August 1959, in fact, the average dividend yield was higher than the yield on government bonds. Since then a 'reverse yield gap', as it is called, has existed. The main reason for the reverse yield gap is the realization by investors that equities offer more protection against the effects of inflation. This has raised share prices relatively and lowered yields.

The dividend yield cannot, however, be regarded as an adequate measure of the cost of equity capital. It fails to take account of the facts that future dividends may be different from the current dividend and that the price of the shares may change. Neither of these considerations is relevant to long-term debt with its fixed interest payments and fixed redemption prices.

Two possible measures of the cost of equity capital are the *earnings yield* and the *dividend yield plus a growth rate*. The earnings yield is calculated as follows:

$$\frac{\text{earnings per ordinary share after tax} \times 100}{\text{market price per ordinary share}}$$

It is usual to express the same relationship in the form of a *price-earnings ratio* (P/E ratio), which is simply the reciprocal of the earnings yield multiplied by 100, i.e.

$$\frac{\text{market price per ordinary share}}{\text{earnings per ordinary share after tax}}$$

In other words, the P/E ratio expresses the multiple of the last reported earnings that the market is willing to pay for the ordinary shares. The higher the P/E ratio (the lower the earnings yield) the more the market thinks of the company and the cheaper the cost of equity capital to the company.

From the extract from the *Financial Times* it can be seen that British Vita's price–earnings ratio on 19 August 1979 was 4·4. The 500 share figure was 6·19.

It is necessary to look a little more closely here at some of the problems of calculating earnings per share (EPS) and hence the price–earnings ratio (P/E). Earnings are calculated *before* the deduction of extraordinary items (discussed on p. 35) but after the deduction of tax and preference dividends. The tax charge, however, depends to some extent on the dividends declared, since there are both constant and variable components in the tax charge.

The statement of standard accounting practice on earnings per share (SSAP 3), which unlike most SSAPs applies only to listed companies, distinguishes between the 'net basis' and the 'nil basis'. The former takes account of both constant and variable components and has the obvious advantage that all the relevant facts are considered. The latter takes account only of the constant components, i.e. it in effect assumes a nil distribution of dividends. Its advantage is that it produces an EPS which is independent of the level of dividend distribution. For most companies, in practice the two bases will give the same result. This is not likely to be the case, however, for companies relying heavily on overseas income. SSAP 3 concludes that companies should use the net basis in their annual reports but should also show the figure arrived at on a nil basis where the difference is material. The *F.T.* calculates P/E ratios on a net basis, putting the resulting figure in brackets if calculation on a nil basis results in a difference of 10 per cent or more. (Imperial Group Ltd is an example of this in the *F.T.* of 20 August 1980.) The *F.T.* calculations also assume an ACT rate of 30 per cent.

The British Vita earnings per share figures are calculated on a net basis. The 1979 calculation is as follows:

$$\text{Basic EPS} = \frac{\text{profit attributable to ordinary shareholders}}{\text{weighted average of ordinary shares in issue during year}}$$
$$= \frac{£6,760,000}{19,847,368} = 34 \cdot 1 \text{p}$$

The P/E ratio is therefore:

$$\frac{\text{market price per share}}{\text{basic EPS}} = \frac{149}{34\cdot1} = 4\cdot4$$

British Vita also publishes a 'fully diluted' EPS figure (32·2p in 1979). This, as note 9 to the profit and loss account explains, is based 'on the assumptions that all outstanding share options had been exercised and the cash subscribed on the exercise of the options had been invested throughout the year at a rate equivalent to the yield on $2\frac{1}{2}$ per cent Consols at the opening Balance Sheet date'.

The final figure which needs to be explained is British Vita's dividend cover, which according to the *F.T.* is 5·6. Since the market is interested in future dividends it prefers to see current dividends reasonably well covered by current earnings. This is some sort of guarantee that the dividend will be at least maintained in future since, if profits fall, there will be past retained profits to draw upon. The *F.T.* measure of dividend cover is

$$\frac{\text{EPS on a maximum basis}}{\text{ordinary dividend per share}}$$

EPS on a maximum basis is yet a third approach to this somewhat elusive concept. It is based on the assumption (seldom, of course, the reality) that a company distributes *all* its profits and is liable to pay ACT on them. This produces a dividend cover of 5·6 as distinct from the 6·6 (= 6,760/1,021) given on page 13 of British Vita's 1979 report.

An alternative approach to the cost of equity capital is to add a growth rate to the dividend yield. If one considers, for example, that British Vita's dividends are likely to grow in future at an average annual rate of 8 per cent, then the cost of its equity capital would be estimated to be 4·8 per cent plus 8 per cent, which equals 12·8 per cent.

An approach to the cost of a company's equity capital strongly favoured in the literature on financial theory is that it is equal to:

$$R_f + \beta[E(\tilde{R}_m) - R_f]$$

where R_f is the return on a riskless security (e.g. a treasury bill), $E(\tilde{R}_m)$ is the expected return on all the securities in the market and β (beta) is a measure of risk.

The meaning and measurement of beta is discussed in the next section.

RISK: BETAS AND GEARING

Risk is of two kinds: market (or systematic) risk and specific (or non-market) risk. Market risk can be quantified as the *beta* of a company's ordinary shares. Beta measures the sensitivity of the share price to movements in the market. British Vita's beta in July 1980 was estimated by the London Business School Risk Measurement Service to be 1·14. A beta of 1·14 means that the share will on average move 1·14 per cent for each 1 per cent move by the market. A share with a beta of 1·0 would on average move in line with the market. Betas tend to range from about 1·5 to about 0·5. The beta of Whitbread & Co. Ltd, for example, was 0·88. Industry betas are also available: 1·05 for plastic and rubber fabricators and 0·99 for breweries in July 1980 if the component companies are weighted by market value.

Specific risk refers to factors specific to a company and is measured as a percentage return per annum. The higher the percentage, the greater the specific risk. Property companies tend to have a high specific risk and investment trusts a low one. Specific risk figures tend to range from 100 per cent down to 10 per cent with an average of 25 per cent. British Vita's and Whitbread's figures were 34 per cent and 20 per cent. Beer is less risky than plastics! (The industry figures were 23 per cent and 19 per cent on a market value weighted basis.)

The distinction between market risk and specific risk is important because it is possible to reduce the latter by diversification (e.g. by holding shares in both plastics and rubber fabricators and in breweries), but market risk cannot be diversified away. Both British Vita and Whitbread are affected by the general state of the economy.

Betas can be measured from either market data ('market betas') or from accounting data ('accounting betas'). The London Business School at present calculates only the former, comparing the monthly returns (dividend yield plus capital appreciation) for the last five years on each share with the corresponding returns on the market index. Betas do, of course, change over time, although most are reasonably stationary.

The more traditional accounting measure of risk is gearing. Companies with the highest betas tend to be highly geared and to come from highly cyclical industries.

Gearing (or 'leverage', as the Americans call it) is the relationship between the funds provided to a company by its ordinary shareholders and the long-term sources of funds carrying a fixed interest charge or dividend (e.g. unsecured loans, debentures and preference shares). The degree of gearing can be measured in terms of either capital or income. A company's capital structure is said to be highly geared when the fixed charges claim an above average proportion of the company's resources of either capital or income.

There is more than one way of defining and calculating a 'gearing ratio'. If we define it as

$$\frac{\text{long-term loans} + \text{preference shares}}{\text{ordinary shareholders' funds}} \times 100\%$$

we can calculate the following ratios from Tables 16 and 17:

	Listed manufacturing and distribution companies	*British Vita*
	%	%
1977	25	22
1978	n.a.	27
1979	n.a.	33

Alternatively, we could add back overdrafts and loans to the numerator on the grounds that, to a large extent, they may be renewed each year and therefore should be treated as long-term sources of funds, even though included under the heading of current liabilities in *Company Finance*.

The relevant figures are also given in Tables 16 and 17. The gearing ratios now become:

	Listed manufacturing and distribution companies	*British Vita*
	%	%
1977	54	26
1978	n.a.	31
1979	n.a.	46

Both the above definitions are based on book values. Market values could (some would say 'should') be used instead if they are available. The definition would now become:

$$\frac{\text{market value of fixed interest securities}}{\text{market value of ordinary share capital}}$$

This has the merit of removing the problem of deferred taxation which has been ignored in our calculations based on book values. Strictly it should be apportioned between the numerator and the denominator depending on the extent to which it represents a liability. The actions of many companies, including British Vita, suggest that most of it was *not* a liability but part of shareholders' funds. If this is the case, the gearing percentages calculated for listed manufacturing and distribution companies are too high.

Whichever way the calculation is made, some companies are more highly geared than others, especially those which have relatively stable profits, and assets, such as land and buildings, which can be specifically identified and are unlikely to fall in value over time, therefore providing good security.

'Times interest earned' is really just a different way of looking at gearing. It is defined as:

$$\frac{\text{profit before interest, tax and extraordinary items}}{\text{interest (gross)}}$$

Using the data on page 13 of the 1979 report, times interest earned can be calculated for British Vita as follows:

$$1977 \quad \frac{6,683}{504} = 13 \cdot 3 \text{ times}$$

$$1978 \quad \frac{7,275}{443} = 16 \cdot 4 \text{ times}$$

$$1979 \quad \frac{10,004}{1,076} = 9 \cdot 3 \text{ times}$$

All the measures show British Vita becoming more highly geared. The major disadvantage of the 'times interest earned' method is that it ignores the existence of reserves, i.e. the retained profits of previous years, upon which the company could call if necessary (if they are in liquid form). The same drawback applies to the 'priority percentages' approach in which the analyst calculates the percentage of earnings that is required to service each category of loan and share capital.

The effect of gearing on profits available to ordinary shareholders can be seen from the following example.

X Ltd is a very highly geared company and Y Ltd a relatively low geared one. Their long-term sources of funds are as follows:

	X	Y
Ordinary share capital (par value)	100,000	200,000
Retained profits	100,000	200,000
Ordinary shareholders' funds	200,000	400,000
10% Debenture	300,000	100,000
	£500,000	£500,000
Gearing ratio (debentures as % of ordinary shareholders' funds)	150%	25%

If profit before interest and tax is £80,000 for both companies, the distributable profit will be as follows, assuming a 50 per cent tax rate:

	X	Y
(a) Profit before interest and tax	80,000	80,000
(b) Debenture interest (gross)	30,000	10,000
	50,000	70,000
Tax at 50%	25,000	35,000
Distributable profit	£25,000	£35,000
Times interest earned (a/b)	2·67	8·00

Distributable profit will be 25 per cent of the par value for Company X and 17·5 per cent for Company Y.

If, however, the profit before interest and tax is £160,000, the position will be as follows:

	X	Y
(a) Profit before interest and tax	160,000	160,000
(b) Debenture interest (gross)	30,000	10,000
	130,000	150,000
Tax at 50%	65,000	75,000
Distributable profit	£65,000	£75,000
Times interest earned (a/b)	5·33	16·00

Distributable profit as a proportion of the par value becomes 65 per cent for Company X and 37·5 per cent for Company Y. Note that whilst profits before interest and tax have doubled, X's distributable profit as a percentage of par value has gone up 2·60 times and Y's 2·14 times. It is clear that gearing enables a company to trade on the equity, as the Americans say, and to increase the ordinary shareholders' return at a faster rate than the increase in profits. The higher the gearing, the greater the relative rate.

Unfortunately the converse also applies. Suppose that the profit before interest and tax falls to £30,000. The position will then be as follows:

	X	Y
(a) Profit before interest and tax	30,000	30,000
(b) Debenture interest (gross)	30,000	10,000
	—	20,000
Tax at 50%	—	10,000
Distributable profit	£ —	£10,000
Times interest earned (a/b)	1·00	3·00

The distributable profit as a proportion of par value of Company X falls to zero and of Company Y to 5 per cent. If profits fell even further, Company X would not be able to pay the debenture interest out of its current profits and would have to call upon past retained profits (reserves). Once these were exhausted it would be in serious trouble. Company Y is in a much better position to meet such an emergency. It must also be remembered, of course, that a company which has tied up its assets too much in fixed assets and stocks may run into similar problems even though its profits have not fallen. Profits are not the same thing as ready cash.

The moral is that companies whose profits are low or likely to fluctuate violently should not be too highly geared. Investors in such companies are running risks and will in any case prefer ordinary shares to fixed-interest debentures. From a company point of view the attraction of a relatively cheap source of funds must be balanced against the risks involved.

DIVIDEND POLICY

How does a company determine the size of the dividend it pays each year, or, putting the same question round the other way, how does a company decide how much of its profits to retain each year? A number of factors are important:

1. the effect of dividend policy on the cost of capital, on the dividend yield and on the dividend cover;
2. government policy;
3. inflation;
4. taxation.

The most convenient source of funds to a company is retained profits. A company which pays very high dividends loses this source and may have to raise money in the capital market. Issues of debentures and other loans usually have a lower cost of capital than either new issues of shares or retained profits but, as we have just seen, there are dangers in a too highly geared capital structure. New issues of shares are more expensive than retained profits because of the issue costs involved.*

On the other hand, most expanding companies will have to go to the market sooner or later, and one of the points potential investors will look at is the dividend record. A company whose dividend has declined or fluctuated violently is not likely to be favourably regarded. For this reason companies prefer to maintain their dividends even if earnings fall.

*Retained profits are not a costless source of funds. They can be regarded as a notional distribution of profits which are immediately re-invested in the company.

On the whole, then, cost of capital considerations push companies towards constant or steadily increasing dividend payouts. Inflation may have the same effect, if the directors of a company feel that the distribution to shareholders ought to keep pace with the decline in the purchasing power of money. It may also have the opposite effect if the directors feel the need to retain a higher proportion of historical cost earnings in order to maintain operating capacity. Two factors which tend to limit the size of the dividend are government policy and taxation. A number of governments since the war, in their efforts to contain rises in wages and prices, have placed statutory limitations on the size of company dividends. In spite of capital gains tax, the British tax system still favours capital increases rather than income increases. There are many shareholders who are more interested in capital gains than dividends.

We are now in a position to look at British Vita's dividend policy. Table 18 gives information about the group's dividend policy for the last five years. It has been adapted from the information given on page 13 of the 1979 Report. All the information is on a historical cost basis. It is interesting to compare the earnings record with the dividend record. Increases in dividends lagged well behind earnings in both 1976 and 1977. There seems little doubt that dividend control was a major reason for this. Government controls operated from 1972 to 1979 and limited the annual increases to varying percentages. The chairman of British Vita comments in his review that 'The abolition of dividend control enabled the Board to declare an interim dividend [for 1979] more commensurate with the performance of the Company ... the proposed final dividend reflects this policy' (App. C, p. 3).

It is the policy of many companies to pay a constant or moderately increased dividend (in money terms) each year, ironing out fluctuations in earnings. This gives shareholders a more certain income and is probably preferred by most of them. British Vita's interim report for the six months ended 30 June 1980 shows a basic earnings per share for the first half of 1980 of 10·7p, compared with 15·1p for the first half of 1979. Nevertheless, the interim dividend per share was increased from 2·4p to 2·6p. It appears that the directors felt that despite the decline in profits, the level of dividend cover was still satisfactory and that during the long period of dividend control dividends had been lower than they might otherwise have been.

TABLE 18: *British Vita Company Ltd: Earnings and Dividends Record, 1975–9*

	1975	1976	1977	1978	1979
Profit attributable to ordinary shareholders	£1,018,000	£1,529,000	£3,890,000	£4,857,000	£6,760,000
Index (1975 = 100)	100	150	382	477	664
Earnings per ordinary share:*					
basic	6·3p	9·8p	19·3p	24·8p	34·1p
fully diluted	6·1p	9·4p	18·3p	23·4p	32·2p
Ordinary dividend	£236,000	£260,000	£290,000	£440,000	£1,021,000
Index (1975 = 100)	100	110	123	186	433
Dividend per ordinary share*	1·21p	1·33p	1·48p	2·33p	5·00p
Dividend cover	4·3	5·9	13·4	11·0	6·6
Index of retail prices (average for calendar year)	135	157	182	197	223

* Adjusted for capitalization issues.

(*Sources:* 1. British Vita Company Ltd, Annual Report and Accounts 1979, page 13. 2. *Accountancy*, July 1980, page 12.)

It is illuminating to compare in Table 18 the dividend per share and the retail price index. In the early years the dividend per share is clearly falling in real terms; it more than catches up in the later years, but still lags behind the increase in historical cost earnings per share.

RIGHTS ISSUES AND BONUS ISSUES

Most issues of new shares are either rights issues or bonus issues. A rights issue is one in which existing shareholders are given a chance to subscribe before anybody else. If they do not wish to do so, they can sell their rights on the market. Rights issues have long been the norm and the Companies Act 1980 makes it obligatory for share issues by public companies to be rights issues.

On 10 September 1980, British Vita announced its first ever rights issue: 5,286,849 new ordinary shares of 25p each were offered on the basis of one new ordinary share for every four ordinary shares held on 1 September 1980. The offer price, fixed as usual a little below the current market price, was 105p per share. 27·5 per cent of the issue was placed with a number of institutions at a price of 16p per share (nil paid) on behalf of certain directors and substantial shareholders who did not wish to take up all their rights.

The effect of the rights issue on British Vita's balance sheet (ignoring the issue costs of approximately £190,000) can be summarized as follows:

	£000
Increase in cash balances	
(5,286,849 × 105p)	5,551
represented by	
Increase in share capital (at par)	
(5,286,849 × 25p)	1,322
Increase in share premium	
(5,286,849 × 80p)	4,229
	5,551

The purpose of the issue was announced by the board of directors to be to enlarge the capital base so that the group retains the flexibility to respond quickly to opportunities as they arise whilst maintaining an appropriate balance between equity and debt. (We have already noticed in this chapter the increase in the group's gearing in recent years.)

When dealings commenced for the nil paid shares the price fluctuated between 10p and 18p. A nil paid price of 16p assumes a market price of 125p before the issue. The value of all the existing shares at this price is $4 \times 5,286,849 \times £1.25 = £26,434,245$. Adding the cash receipts from the new shares ($5,286,849 \times £1.05 = £5,551,191$) gives a new total of £31,985,436. Dividing this by the new number of shares ($5 \times 5,286,849 = 26,434,245$) results in a new value per share of 121p (i.e. 105p + 16p).

An existing shareholder who sells his rights for 16p will be no worse off than one who takes up his rights at 105p. Assume a shareholder with 4,000 shares and £1,050 in cash. If he uses the cash to take up his rights, he will have 5,000 shares valued at 121p each, i.e. £6,050. If he sells his rights for 16p per new share, he will have 4,000 shares valued £4,840 and £1,210 in cash (the original £1,050 plus £160 from the sale), i.e. £6,050. A shareholder who takes no action would have his rights automatically sold in the market and would receive the proceeds net of expenses of sale.

A bonus issue (also known as a 'scrip issue', a 'capitalization issue' and, in the United States, a 'stock dividend') is simply a means of turning reserves into share capital. To clear up the misunderstandings which can arise from this, it is helpful to use a simple example. Consider a company whose summarized balance sheet is as follows:

Assets	150,000	Ordinary share capital (40,000 shares of £1 each)	40,000
less Liabilities	50,000	Reserves	60,000
	£100,000		£100,000

The company decides to make a bonus issue of one new share for two old shares. The balance sheet will now look like this:

Assets	150,000	Ordinary share capital (60,000 shares of £1 each)	60,000
less Liabilities	50,000	Reserves	40,000
	£100,000		£100,000

All that has happened is a book entry. In order to increase the ordinary share capital from £40,000 to £60,000, the accountant has decreased the reserves from £60,000 to £40,000. The shareholders have not received any cash, only more paper. Are they any better off? In principle no; the market price *per share* might be expected to fall proportionately. It may not do so, partly because unrelated factors may be affecting share prices at the same time, partly because the issue may have drawn favourable attention to the future prospects of the company. Of course, if the company announces at the same time that the total amount to be paid out in dividends to shareholders will be increased then the shareholders really are better off and the market price will tend to rise.

CONVERTIBLE LOAN STOCK

So far in this book we have drawn a rather rigid dividing line between debenture-holders, who are merely long-term creditors of a company, and shareholders, who are its owners. It will have been apparent, however, that preference share capital has some of the characteristics of long-term debt. Another hybrid security of importance is the convertible loan.

The annual report of Whitbread and Co. Ltd, for example, includes the following item among the long-term loan capital:

$11\frac{1}{2}$% convertible unsecured loan stock 1990/95 – £12·97 million

The attraction of such stock to an investor is that it enables him to buy a fixed interest stock which he can later change into ordinary shares if he so wishes. Whether he will make the conversion or not depends, of course, on the relationship between the market price of the ordinary shares and the conversion price at the conversion date. The investor's hope is that he has found a cheaper way of buying the ordinary shares than direct purchase. The disadvantage to him is that the rate of interest offered on a convertible loan is less than that on a 'straight' loan.

Why should a company issue convertible stock? There are at least two possibilities:

1. the company wants to issue debt and adds the convertibility as an added attraction;

2. the company would prefer to issue equity but feels that the price of its ordinary shares is temporarily depressed. By setting the conversion price higher than the current price, the management can, if its expectations are fulfilled, effectively make a share issue at the desired price.

The possible disadvantages to the company are that either the market price fails to rise and it is saddled with unwanted debt, or that the market price rises so quickly that it finds itself in effect selling equity more cheaply than it need have done. As already noted, the existence of convertible loan stock dilutes the basic earnings per share.

LEASING

Instead of borrowing money to buy fixed assets, a company may decide to lease them, i.e. to enter into a long-term contract which allows it the use of the asset (but does not give it the ownership) in return for a periodic rental. Early termination of the lease is penalized. Sometimes the company already owns the assets and raises cash by selling them and then leasing them back. This is known as sale-and-leaseback.

The effect in either case is similar to an issue of long-term debt and it should be regarded and analysed as such. One important difference is that neither the leased asset nor the long-term liability to pay the rentals are as yet shown in the balance sheet, although they may be disclosed in footnotes. British Vita discloses lease rentals paid of £468,000 (App. C, p. 18, note 2).

These omissions can lead to misleading ratios and many accountants now believe that the capitalized value of the lease rentals should be shown in the balance sheet as both an asset and a liability.

As in all financing decisions, the effect on the tax payable by the company is an important factor in deciding whether or not to use leasing. If equipment is bought out of borrowed money, the company will be entitled to the capital allowances described in chapter 3 and the interest on the loan will be tax-deductible. If the equipment is leased the lessor will receive the benefit of the capital allowances but the lessee's annual taxable income will be reduced by the amount of the lease rental. It is not possible to state in general terms whether the tax effect will be favourable or unfavourable to the prospective lessee. Each case has to be analysed separately.

9. Summary and Reading Guide

The reader who has come this far has already learned a great deal about the annual reports of companies, about financial statements and about accounting and finance. The purpose of this chapter is to summarize what has been learned and to make suggestions about further reading.

COMPANIES

Chapter 1 was mainly about companies, the most important form of business organization in modern Britain. Nearly 98 per cent of all companies are private but public companies are of greater economic significance. It is with public companies, and especially with those that are listed on the stock exchange, that investors are mainly concerned. Published annual reports are typically those of groups of companies, consisting of a holding company, subsidiaries, sub-subsidiaries and associated companies.

Company law, partly as a result of a programme of E.E.C. harmonization, is in a state of change. At the date of writing companies are governed by the Companies Acts 1948 to 1980 and the relevant case law. Of the many texts on the subject two can be especially recommended: Goldberg, Leigh and Josse, Northey and Leigh's *Introduction to Company Law* (Butterworths, 2nd edn, 1980) and Gower, Cronin, Easson and Wedderburn, *Gower's Principles of Modern Company Law* (Stevens, 4th edn, 1979).

FINANCIAL STATEMENTS

Chapter 2 dealt with financial statements. The three most important statements are:

1. *the balance sheet*, which shows the assets, the liabilities and the shareholders' funds at a particular date;
2. *the profit and loss account* (or income statement), which shows for an accounting period the revenues, expenses, net profit (before and after taxation) and often also the distribution of the profit; and
3. *the source and application of funds statement* (funds statement), which shows the sources and uses of funds of a company over the same accounting period.

Assets are classified into *fixed* and *current* and liabilities into *current* and *long-term*. The excess of current assets over current liabilities is the working capital of a company. The fixed assets are depreciated over their estimated economic lives, depreciation in its accounting sense normally referring to the allocation over time of the cost less estimated scrap value.

Long-term sources of funds of companies can be divided into *loan capital* (e.g. debentures) on the one hand and *shareholders' funds* (share capital and reserves) on the other. There is an important distinction between preference shares, usually carrying a fixed dividend rate and having priority in a winding up, and ordinary shares, which form the *equity* of the company. The par or face value of a share is not necessarily the same as its issue price (issues are often made at a premium) or its market price.

The profit and loss account is drawn up from the point of view of the shareholders. Much the same information can be used to prepare a statement of value added which shows how wealth has been created by the operations of the group and how that wealth has been allocated.

The source and application of funds statement demonstrates among other things the difference between increases in profit and increases in cash balances. Cash flow is a rather imprecise term often meaning simply net profit plus depreciation and other items not involving the movement of funds.

A good introductory book on accounting and financial statements is C. Nobes, *Introduction to Financial Accounting* (Allen & Unwin, 1980). More specialized are T. A. Lee, *Company Financial Reporting* (Nelson, 1976) and G. A. Lee, *Modern Financial Accounting* (Nelson, 3rd edn, 1981). The legal requirements of the Companies Acts 1948 to 1980 insofar as they relate to accounting are conveniently summarized in the Institute of Chartered Accountants in England and Wales, *Guide to the Accounting Requirements of the Companies Acts 1948–1980* (Gee, 1980).

TAXATION

Chapter 3 dealt briefly with taxation and audit. Companies pay corporation tax, not income tax. Taxable income is measured in much the same way as accounting profit, with the two major exceptions of capital allowances (which replace depreciation) and stock appreciation relief. The corporation tax rate refers to a financial year which ends on 31 March but companies are assessed on the basis of their own accounting periods.

Under the U.K.'s imputation system, companies pay advance corporation tax when a dividend is paid and the shareholder receives a tax credit.

In general, taxable income is less than accounting profit. The total amount of taxation so 'deferred' is disclosed in the notes and included in the balance sheet to the extent that it is a liability.

Books on taxation tend to be written either for accountants (lots of figures), for lawyers (lots of case law) or for economists (lots of diagrams). Two books rather more readable and stimulating than most are J. A. Kay and M. A. King, *The British Tax System* (Oxford University Press, 2nd edn, 1980) and S. James and C. Nobes, *The Economics of Taxation* (Philip Allan, 1978). *The Workbook for the Economics of Taxation* is revised annually and contains up-to-date details of tax rates and allowances.

AUDIT

The main function of the auditors of a company is to report to the shareholders whether in their opinion the financial statements show a true and fair view. A good introductory book is T. A. Lee, *Com-*

pany Auditing: Concepts and Practices (Institute of Chartered Accountants of Scotland, 1972).

ACCOUNTING STANDARDS AND INFLATION

Accounting standards and inflation accounting were discussed in chapter 4.

In Britain, decisions about disclosure, presentation and valuation are mainly in the hands of the government, through company law, and the accountancy profession, through statements of standard accounting practice issued by the Accounting Standards Committee.

Financial statements have traditionally been based on historical cost modified by prudence but the high rates of inflation of the 1970s have led to the introduction of current cost accounting in addition. This is still being tested in practice but is likely to lead to more relevant financial statements.

As noted in chapter 5, all extant accounting standards and exposure drafts are reproduced in *Accounting Standards*, revised annually and published by the Institute of Chartered Accountants in England and Wales. P. R. A. Kirkman's *Accounting under Inflationary Conditions* (Allen & Unwin, 2nd edn, 1978) deals expertly with most aspects of inflation accounting. The most important theoretical work is E. O. Edwards and P. W. Bell, *The Theory and Measurement of Business Income* (University of California Press, 1961). A number of classic articles are brought together in R. H. Parker and G. C. Harcourt, *Readings in the Concept and Measurement of Income* (Cambridge University Press, 1969).

TOOLS OF ANALYSIS

Chapter 5 was concerned with defining and explaining the uses and limitations of ratios, percentages and yields as tools for the analysis of financial statements. George Foster's *Financial Statement Analysis* (Prentice-Hall, 1978) is a very thorough treatment of the subject. There are relevant chapters in the books by Nobes, G. A. Lee and T. A. Lee (1976) already referred to, and in John Sizer, *An Insight into Management Accounting* (Penguin, 2nd edn, 1979).

PROFITABILITY AND RETURN ON INVESTMENT

Profitability and return on investment were discussed in chapter 6, in which the relationships between sales, profits and assets were considered.

LIQUIDITY AND CASH FLOWS

In chapter 7 it was pointed out that a company must be liquid as well as profitable and that making profits is not the same as accumulating cash. It was shown that the best way to control liquidity from inside the company is by means of a cash budget. The external analyst uses the current ratio and the quick ratio as rather cruder measures. Other indicators of liquidity are the defensive interval, the average collection period and stock turnover. The extreme case of illiquidity is insolvency; some success has been achieved in predicting this by means of financial ratios.

SOURCES OF FUNDS AND CAPITAL STRUCTURE

Chapter 8 discussed sources of funds and capital structure. It was pointed out that shareholders are still the most important source of long-term funds, especially through the medium of retained profits, but that loan capital has steadily gained in importance in recent years. This has led to higher gearing ratios.

The problem of capital structure is to obtain the best mix of debt and equity. Factors to be considered are cost, risk, control, acceptability and transferability. It was argued that either the earnings yield (reciprocal of the price-earnings ratio) or the dividend yield plus a growth rate are better measures of the cost of equity than the dividend yield itself. The imputation system of corporate taxation has greatly complicated the calculation of measures of earnings per share.

Risk can be approached through traditional measures of gearing or through the calculation of *betas* which quantify the market risk of a share as distinguished from its specific risk.

In deciding on its dividend policy, a company looks at its effects on the cost of capital, on dividend yield and on dividend cover and has to take account of government policy, inflation and taxation. Most companies try to pay a constant or moderately increased dividend (in money terms) each year, ironing out fluctuations in earnings.

Rights issues give existing shareholders the first chance to subscribe to new issues. They are distinguished from bonus issues where the existing shareholders receive extra shares without further subscription.

The chapter ended with brief references to two other sources of funds: convertible loan stock and leasing.

There are a number of good books on the topics discussed in chapters 6, 7 and 8. Examples are R. J. Briston, *The Stock Exchange and Investment Analysis* (Allen & Unwin, 3rd edn, 1975), M. Firth, *Investment Analysis* (Harper & Row, 1975), J. R. Franks and J. E. Broyles, *Modern Managerial Finance* (Wiley, 1979), J. M. Samuels and F. M. Wilkes, *The Management of Company Finance*, (Nelson, 3rd edn, 1980) and (with an American institutional background) J. C. Van Horne, *Financial Management and Policy* (Prentice Hall, 5th edn, 1980).

PERSONAL INVESTMENT

This book has not dealt, except incidentally, with problems of personal investment. Its primary purpose has been to explain and interpret company annual reports and financial statements, not to advise the reader on how to invest his money. It is not perhaps out of place, however, to conclude by recommending two books which do this: *The Which? Book of Money* (Consumers' Association, 1980) and *Pears Guide to the World of Money* (Pelham Books, 1981).

Appendix A. Debits and Credits (Double Entry)

Welche Vorteile gewährt die doppelte Buchhaltung dem Kaufmanne!
JOHANN WOLFGANG VON GOETHE, *Wilhelm Meisters Lehrjahre*, I, x.

Most people know that accountants are concerned with debits and credits. Since it is possible to learn quite a lot about accounting and finance without using these terms, it has not been thought necessary to explain their meaning within the body of this book. Very little extra effort is required, however, to master double entry, so a brief explanation is given in this appendix.

It will be remembered that the following symbols were used in chapter 2:

a = assets	r = revenues (e.g. sales, fees)
l = liabilities	e = expenses other than taxation
c = shareholders' funds	t = taxation
s = share capital	d = dividends
p = retained profits	Δ = net increase in

The identity for any balance sheet is

$$a = l + c$$

which can be expanded to

$$a = l + s + p$$

An increase on the left-hand side of the identity is called a debit (abbreviated to Dr.), an increase on the right-hand side a credit (abbreviated to Cr.). Similarly, decreases on the left-hand side are credits and decreases on the right-hand side are debits. Debit and credit are used here as technical terms and should not be confused with any other meanings of these words.

In chapter 2 we showed that an increase in retained profits (Δp) is equal to revenue less expenses, tax and dividends:

$$\Delta p = r - e - t - d$$

Now, since increases in retained profits are credits it follows that increases in revenues are also credits, whereas increases in expenses, taxes and dividends must be debits. Conversely, decreases in revenues are debits and decreases in expenses, taxes and dividends are credits.

We can sum up the rules as follows:

DEBITS ARE:		CREDITS ARE:	
Increases in:	assets	*Increases in:*	liabilities
	expenses		share capital
	taxes		retained profits
	dividends	revenues	
Decreases in:	liabilities	*Decreases in:*	assets
	share capital		expenses
	retained profits		taxes
	revenues		dividends

It seems curious at first sight that both increases in assets and expenses are debits. In fact, assets and expenses are much more closely linked than is usually realized. If a company buys for cash a machine which is expected to last ten years, it is rightly regarded as having acquired the asset machine (increase in machines, therefore debit 'machines') in exchange for the asset cash (decrease in cash, therefore credit 'cash'). Suppose, however, that technological change is so rapid that these machines have an economic life of only one year or less. Then, if the accounting period is one year, the machine can be regarded as an expense of the period (therefore, debit 'machine expense', credit 'cash'). Thus, in one sense, an asset is merely an expense paid for in advance which needs to be spread over several accounting periods in the form of depreciation.

The system of debits and credits is referred to as double entry, since maintenance of the accounting identity ($a = l + c$ in its simplest form) requires that any increase or decrease in one item be balanced by a corresponding increase of decrease in another item or items. There are always two sides to any transaction. Suppose, for example, that a company decreases its cash by £100. The other side of the transaction might be:

1. an increase in another asset such as a machine (so, debit 'machine', credit 'cash');

2. a decrease in a liability, such as a trade creditor (so, debit 'creditor', credit 'cash');

3. an increase in a negative capital item such as expenses, taxes or dividends (so, debit 'expenses', 'taxes' or 'dividends', credit 'cash').

Note that cash is always credited (since the asset cash has been decreased) and that a negative credit is the same as a debit (and a negative debit the same as a credit).

Appendix B. Glossary of Accounting and Financial Terms

This glossary serves two purposes:

1. to collect in alphabetical order various definitions, descriptions and explanations scattered throughout the text;
2. to provide certain *additional* information, especially concerning those matters which must by law be disclosed in the published financial statements of companies.

ACCELERATED DEPRECIATION: The writing off of depreciation, e.g. for tax purposes, at a faster rate than is justified by the rate of use of the asset concerned.

ACCOUNTING CONCEPTS: The assumptions underlying the periodic financial statements of business enterprises.

ACCOUNTING IDENTITY (or EQUATION): Another name for the Balance Sheet Identity (q.v.).

ACCOUNTING PERIOD: The period between two balance sheets, usually a year from the point of view of shareholders and taxation authorities. Corporation tax is assessed on the basis of a company's accounting period.

ACCOUNTING POLICIES: The accounting methods selected and consistently followed by a business enterprise. Most companies publish a list of accounting policies in their annual reports.

ACCOUNTING REFERENCE PERIOD: A company's accounting period as notified to the Registrar of Companies (31 March applies if notification not given).

ACCOUNTING STANDARDS: *see* Statements of Standard Accounting Practice.

ACCOUNTING STANDARDS COMMITTEE (ASC): A committee established by the major professional accountancy bodies in Britain to issue Statements of Standard Accounting Practice (q.v.).

ACCOUNTS PAYABLE: Amounts owing by a company; usually called creditors in Britain.

ACCOUNTS RECEIVABLE: Amounts owing to a company; usually called debtors in Britain.

ACCRUALS: The accounting concept that revenues are recognized as they are earned or incurred, not as money is received (accrual basis of accounting as distinct from cash basis).

ACCUMULATED DEPRECIATION: The cumulative amount of depreciation written off a fixed asset at a balance sheet date.

ACID TEST: Another name for the Quick Ratio (q.v.).

ADVANCE CORPORATION TAX (ACT): Tax payable in advance when a company pays a dividend; the amount is tied to the basic rate of income tax. ACT is normally recoverable. The difference between the total corporation tax liability and ACT is known as Mainstream Corporation Tax (q.v.).

AKTIENGESELLSCHAFT (AG): The approximate German equivalent of the British public company.

ALLOTMENT: The allocation of shares by the directors of a company following applications for them by intending shareholders.

AMORTIZATION: The writing off over a period of an asset or a liability. Sometimes used synonymously with Depreciation (q.v.).

ANNUAL GENERAL MEETING (AGM): Meeting of the members (shareholders) of a company held annually at intervals of not more than fifteen months (but first AGM may be held within eighteen months of formation). Usual business transacted: reception of directors' report and accounts; declaration of dividend; election of directors; appointment of auditors.

ANNUAL REPORT: Report made annually by the directors of a company to its shareholders. Its contents are largely determined by company law and statements of standard accounting practice.

ANNUAL RETURN: Document which must be completed within forty-two days of the Annual General Meeting (q.v.) and forthwith forwarded to the Registrar of Companies (q.v.). Main contents are:

1. address of registered office;

2. addresses where registers of members and debenture-holders are kept;

3. summary of share capital and debentures, giving number of issued shares of each class, the consideration for them, details of shares not fully paid-up, etc.;

4. particulars of mortgages and charges;

5. list of names and addresses of past and present shareholders giving number of shares held and particulars of transfers;

6. names, addresses and occupations of directors and secretaries (and nationality of directors).

Copies of the financial statements, directors' report and auditors' report must be annexed to the return.

All the above can be inspected at the Companies Registries in Cardiff or Edinburgh on payment of a fee.

APPLICATION MONEY: The amount per share or unit of stock payable on application for a new issue of shares or debentures.

ARTICLES OF ASSOCIATION: The internal regulations of a company. Usually deal with: rights of various classes of shares; calls on shares; transfer, transmission and forfeiture of shares; alteration of share capital; general meetings (notice, proceedings); votes and proxies; directors (powers, duties, disqualification, rotation, proceedings); dividends and reserves; accounts; capitalization of profits; audit; winding up; and similar matters.

ASSET: Any property tangible or intangible from which future benefits are expected, and of which a company has a legal right of use as a result of a past or present transaction. Examples: machinery, stock-in-trade, debtors, cash, goodwill.

ASSOCIATED COMPANY: A company over which an investing group or company has a significant influence and in which the investor is *either* a partner in a joint venture or consortium *or* has a long-term and substantial interest.

AUDITORS: Independent experts who report to the shareholders of a company their opinion on the truth and fairness of published financial statements. Their remuneration (including expenses) must be disclosed in the published profit and loss account.

Auditors must either be members of a body of accountants established in the U.K. and recognized by the Board of Trade, or be authorized by the Board of Trade to be appointed. The auditor must not be an officer or servant of the company or of a company in the group; a body corporate; or a partner or employee of an officer or servant of the company or a company in the group.

AUTHORIZED SHARE CAPITAL: The maximum share capital which the directors of a company can issue at any given time. Disclosed in the balance sheet or the notes.

AVERAGE COLLECTION PERIOD: The speed at which a company collects its debts:

$$\frac{\text{debtors} \times 365}{\text{credit sales}} \text{ days}$$

BALANCE SHEET: Statement of the assets, liabilities and shareholders' funds of a company at a particular date. The Companies Acts provide that share capital, reserves, provisions, liabilities, fixed assets, current assets and other assets must be separately identified and that every balance sheet shall give a true and fair view of the state of affairs of the company.

BALANCE SHEET IDENTITY (or EQUATION): The identity: assets *equals* liabilities *plus* shareholders' funds.

BEARER SECURITIES: Debentures or shares transferable by simple delivery.

BETA: A measure of the market (or systematic) risk of a company's shares, i.e. the sensitivity of the share price to movements in the market.

BONDS: Fixed interest securities such as government loans or (in the U.S.A.) company debentures.

BONUS SHARES: Shares issued to existing shareholders without further payment on their part. Also referred to as a scrip issue, a capitalization issue and (in the U.S.A.) a stock dividend.

BOOK VALUE: The monetary amount of an asset as stated in the balance sheet and books of account.

CALLED-UP SHARE CAPITAL: The amount of the Issued Share Capital (q.v.) which has been called up, i.e. the amounts shareholders have been asked to pay to date. Equal to the paid-up share capital unless there are calls in arrear or calls have been paid in advance.

CALLS: Demands by a company for part or all of the balance owed on partly paid shares.

CAPITAL ALLOWANCES: In effect, the depreciation allowable for tax purposes. May differ quite substantially from that charged in the published financial statements.

CAPITAL EXPENDITURE: Expenditure on fixed assets. The amount of contracts for capital expenditure not provided for and the amount of capital expenditure authorized by the directors but not contracted for must be disclosed.

CAPITAL GAINS TAX: A tax on individuals. Companies pay corporation tax on their capital gains, not capital gains tax.

CAPITAL REDEMPTION RESERVE FUND: When Preference Shares (q.v.) are redeemed otherwise than out of a new issue of shares, a sum equal to their nominal value must be transferred to an account with this name. For most purposes the Fund is treated as if it were Share Capital (q.v.).

CAPITAL STRUCTURE: The composition of a company's sources of funds, especially long-term.

CAPITALIZATION ISSUE: *see* Bonus Issue.

CASH BUDGET: A plan of future cash receipts and payments based on specified assumptions concerning sales growth, credit terms, etc.

CASH FLOW: An imprecise term; usually defined as net profit plus depreciation and other items not involving the movement of funds, i.e. total funds generated from operations. Not the same as the change in cash balance during the year.

CHAIRMAN'S REVIEW (or STATEMENT): Statement made by the chairman of a company at its annual general meeting and often included in the annual report. There are no legal regulations relating to its contents but it often contains interesting and useful information.

CLOSE COMPANY: A company resident in the U.K. which is under the control of five or fewer participators, or of participators who are directors. Introduced by the Finance Act 1965.

COMMON STOCK: American term for Ordinary Shares (q.v.).

COMPANY: Rather imprecise term implying corporate activity. This book deals with companies registered under the Companies Acts. The liability of such companies is limited except in the case of unlimited companies.

COMPARABILITY: An accounting concept which emphasizes ease of comparison of the financial statements of different companies at a point in time.

CONSERVATISM: *see* Prudence.

CONSISTENCY: An accounting concept which emphasizes consistency of Accounting Policies (q.v.) over time for a particular company rather than Comparability (q.v.) of the financial statements of different companies at any one point in time.

CONSOLIDATED BALANCE SHEET: Balance sheet of a group of companies as distinct from the holding company only.

CONSOLIDATED PROFIT AND LOSS ACCOUNT: Profit and loss account of a group of companies as distinct from the holding company only. A holding company need not publish its own profit and loss account as well if the consolidated profit and loss account discloses the requisite details (*see* Profit and Loss Account) and also discloses what portion of the consolidated profit (or loss) has been dealt with in its accounts.

CONSOLIDATION OF SHARE CAPITAL: Combination of shares into larger units (e.g. combining two £0.50 shares into one of £1).

CONTINGENCIES: Conditions which exist at the balance sheet date the outcome of which will be confirmed only on the occurrence or non-occurrence of one or more uncertain events. Contingent liabilities must be disclosed as a footnote to the balance sheet.

CONVERTIBLE LOAN STOCK: Loan stock which may be converted at the option of the holder at a future date or dates into ordinary stock at given price ratios.

CORPORATION TAX: A tax on companies; not payable by individuals. The rate may vary; for 1979/80 it was 52 per cent. There is a lower rate for small profits.

COST OF CAPITAL: The cost to a company of obtaining funds for investment.

COST OF SALES ADJUSTMENT (COSA): An adjustment made in Current Cost Accounting (q.v.) in order to base the cost of goods sold on the cost current at the time of consumption instead of the time of purchase.

COUPON RATE OF INTEREST: The rate of interest on the par value of a debenture or bond. Not necessarily equal to the effective rate.

CREDIT: *see* Double Entry.

CREDITORS: Amounts owing by a company resulting from (for example) the purchase of goods. The American term is 'accounts payable'.

CUM: Latin for 'with'. A price so quoted includes any dividend (div.), bonus issue, rights or other distribution.

CUMULATIVE PREFERENCE SHARES: Preference shares entitled to be paid the arrears of their dividend before any dividend is paid on the ordinary shares. Any arrears must be disclosed as a note to the balance sheet.

CURRENT ASSETS: Those assets which are either already cash or can reasonably be expected to become cash within one year from the date of the balance sheet. Examples: debtors, stock-in-trade. If the directors believe that any of the current assets will not realize their balance sheet values in the ordinary course of business this fact must be disclosed. The alternative terms 'circulating assets' and 'floating assets' are now obsolete.

CURRENT COST ACCOUNTING: A system of accounting in which assets are stated at the Value to the Business (q.v.) and current costs instead of historical costs are matched against revenues.

CURRENT COST RESERVE: A reserve to which is transferred an amount equal to all the adjustments necessary to convert historical cost accounts into current cost accounts.

CURRENT LIABILITIES: Liabilities (q.v.) which are expected to have been paid within one year from the date of the balance sheet (e.g. trade creditors, proposed final dividend, current taxation).

CURRENT PURCHASING POWER ACCOUNTING: A system of accounting which adjusts historical cost accounts for changes in the general price level.

CURRENT RATIO: Ratio of current assets to current liabilities. A measure of liquidity.

CURRENT TAXATION: Tax payable within one year from the date of the balance sheet.

DEBENTURE DISCOUNT: Arises from issuing debentures at less than their par value. Disclosed in balance sheet to extent that not written off.

DEBENTURES: Loans, usually but not necessarily secured on the assets of the company. Usually redeemable but may be irredeemable.

DEBIT: *see* Double Entry.

DEBTORS: Amounts owing to the company, e.g. from the sale of goods. The American term is 'accounts receivable'. Usually shown in balance sheets net of an allowance ('provision') for doubtful debts.

DEFENSIVE INTERVAL: A measure of how many days operating expenses can be paid out of quick assets.

DEFERRED ASSET: An asset representing cash receivable outside the forthcoming accounting period.

DEFERRED TAXATION: Taxation arising from the excess in the current year of accounting profit over taxable income. The potential amount of deferred taxation payable is disclosed in the notes. Under the 'liability' method, only deferred taxation which is likely to have to be paid within three years is included in the balance sheet.

DEPRECIATION: A measure of the wearing out, consumption or other loss of value of a fixed asset arising from use, effluxion of time or obsolescence through technology and market changes. Amount of depreciation charged must be disclosed. Usually measured by allocating either the historical or replacement cost less scrap value of the asset on a straight-line or reducing balance basis. The accumulated (provision for) depreciation is deducted from the cost in the balance sheet to give the net book value. Depreciation is neither a source nor a use of funds.

DEPRECIATION ADJUSTMENT: An adjustment made in Current Cost Accounting (q.v.) in order to base depreciation on current replacement cost instead of historical cost.

DILUTION: The decrease in control and/or earnings per share suffered by existing shareholders when a new issue of shares is wholly or partly subscribed to by new shareholders.

DIRECTIVE: A statement adopted by the Council of Ministers on the proposal of the Commission of the European Communities. Directives are implemented through national legislation.

DIRECTORS' EMOLUMENTS: The following information must be disclosed:

1. amounts received by directors and past directors as emoluments, pensions and compensation in respect of services as directors and as executives;

2. emoluments of chairman and of highest paid director (if greater than chairman's);

3. number of directors whose emoluments amounted to not more than £5,000, number whose emoluments amounted to between £5,001 and £10,000 and so on in bands of £5,000;

4. number of directors who waived their emoluments and the aggregate amount waived;

5. number of employees in U.K. whose emoluments exceeded £20,000 but were not more than £25,000, exceeded £25,000 but were not more than £30,000 and so on in bands of £5,000.

(*Note*: (2) and (3) do not apply to anyone whose duties were discharged wholly or mainly outside the U.K. If aggregate of directors' earnings does not exceed £40,000 no disclosure need be made thereof.)

DIRECTORS' REPORT: Annual report by the directors of a company to the shareholders which must contain, *inter alia*, details of:

1. the principal activities of the company and any significant change in them during the financial year;

2. any significant change in the fixed assets of the group during the financial year and any substantial and significant difference between the market value and the balance sheet value of interests in land;

3. shares, stock or debentures issued during the financial year;

4. interest of any director in any significant contract entered into by the company;

5. group turnover and profit (or loss) before tax divided among classes of business that differ substantially (excepting banking and discounting business and any company which is not part of a group and whose turnover does not exceed £1,000,000);

6. amount (if more than £50) given by group for political or charitable purposes;

7. amounts recommended to be paid as dividends, and transfers to reserves;

8. exports (unless group turnover less than £1,000,000 or directors satisfy Department of Trade that not in national interest to disclose);

9. names of directors;

10. any arrangement to which company is party to enable directors to acquire benefits through acquisition of shares or debentures of the company or any other company;

11. each director's interest in shares or debentures of the company or other companies in the group;

12. average number of employees in U.K. under contracts of service of the group in each week together with their annual aggregate remuneration (not required where less than 100 employees or if company wholly owned subsidiary of company incorporated in Great Britain);

13. arrangements for securing the health, safety and welfare at work of employees.

DISCOUNTED CASH FLOW: The present value of future cash receipts and payments; i.e. their value after taking into account the expected delay in receiving or paying them.

DISTRIBUTABLE RESERVES: A company's accumulated realized profits so far as not previously distributed or capitalized, *less* its accumulated realized losses so far as not previously written off in a reduction or reorganization of capital. Public companies may only pay a dividend if the net assets are not less than the aggregate of the called-up share capital and undistributable reserves.

DIVIDEND: That part of the profits of a company which is distributed to the shareholders. May be interim (paid during the financial year) or final (recommended by the directors for approval by the shareholders at annual general meeting). The proposed final dividend is shown in the balance sheet as a current liability.

DIVIDEND CONTROL: Limitation of dividend payments by government regulation.

DIVIDEND COVER: The ratio between Earnings Per Share (q.v.) and the ordinary dividend per share.

DIVIDEND POLICY: A company's policy on how to divide its profits between distributions to shareholders (dividends) and re-investment (retained profits).

DIVIDEND YIELD: The relationship between the ordinary dividend and the market price per ordinary share, usually multiplied by $10/7$ to allow for a tax credit.

DOUBLE ENTRY: A system of recording transactions based on the Balance Sheet Identity (q.v.). Broadly, increases in assets and decreases in liabilities and capital items (including expenses) are *debits*, and increases in liabilities and capital items (including revenues) and decreases in assets are *credits*.

EARNINGS PER SHARE (EPS): Net profit attributable to the ordinary shareholder (before tax, extraordinary items and preference dividends) divided by the number of ordinary shares. May be calculated on a net, nil or maximum basis (qq.v.). The 'basic' EPS may be supplemented by a 'fully diluted' EPS to allow for share options and convertible loan stock.

EARNINGS YIELD: The relationship between the earnings per ordinary share and the market price per ordinary share. The reciprocal of the Price–Earnings Ratio (q.v.) multiplied by 100.

EQUITY METHOD: Method of accounting for investments in associated companies.

EQUITY SHARE CAPITAL: Defined by the Companies Acts as any issued share capital which has unlimited rights to participate in either the distribution of dividends or capital. Often more narrowly defined to mean Ordinary Shares (q.v.) only.

EX: Latin for 'without'. A price so quoted excludes any dividend (div.), bonus issue, rights or other distribution.

EXCEPTIONAL ITEMS: Items exceptional on account of size and incidence which derive from the ordinary activities of a business. Compare Extraordinary Items.

EXEMPT PRIVATE COMPANY: No longer exists. Before the Companies Act 1967 was essentially a family company with the privilege of not having to publish its financial statements.

EXPOSURE DRAFT: A draft Statement of Standard Accounting Practice (q.v.) published for comment by interested parties.

EXTRAORDINARY ITEMS: Items which derive from events or transactions outside the ordinary activities of a business and which are both material and expected not to recur frequently or regularly. Compare Exceptional Items.

FINANCIAL RATIO: Relationship among items in financial statements.

FINANCIAL STATEMENTS: Statements showing the financial position (balance sheet), profit for a period (profit and loss account), and sources and uses of funds for a period (source and application of funds statement) of a company. Some companies also publish a statement of added value.

FINANCIAL YEAR: Runs for corporation tax purposes from 1 April to the following 31 March.

FIRST-YEAR ALLOWANCE: The amount deductible for tax purposes during the first year of life of plant and machinery.

FIXED ASSETS: Those assets which are intended for use on a continuing basis for the purpose of an undertaking's activities. In general there must be shown:

    1. method or methods used to arrive at the amount of fixed assets under each heading;

    2. for each class of asset the aggregate cost or valuation and the

accumulated depreciation since the date of acquisition or valuation;

3. years of valuation and the amounts (also, if valued during financial year, name of valuers or their qualifications, and the bases of valuations);

4. aggregate of additions and aggregate of disposals during the year;

5. which land is freehold and which is leasehold: latter to be subdivided into long leases (not less than 50 years unexpired) and short leases.

FIXED CHARGE: A charge which is attached to some specific asset or assets.

FIXED OVERHEADS: Those overheads whose amount remains constant over the usual range of activity.

FLAT YIELD: A Yield (q.v.) which does not take account of the redemption value of a security.

FLOATING CHARGE: A charge which is not attached to any specific asset but to all assets or to a class of assets.

FOREIGN COMPANY: A company incorporated outside Great Britain.

FOREIGN CURRENCIES: The financial statements of foreign subsidiaries must be translated into sterling before they can be included in the consolidated statements. The method of translation must be disclosed.

FRANKED INVESTMENT INCOME: Dividends received by one British company from another, with the addition of the related tax credit. The dividend and the credit can be passed on to the shareholders of the recipient company without payment of corporation tax.

FUNDS STATEMENT: *see* Source and Application of Funds, Statement of.

GEARING: The relationship between the funds provided to a company by its ordinary shareholders and the long-term sources of funds carrying a fixed interest charge or dividend.

GEARING ADJUSTMENT: An adjustment in current cost accounts intended to show the benefit to shareholders of the use of long-term debt, measured by the extent to which the net operating assets are financed by borrowing.

GESELLSCHAFT MIT BESCHRÄNKTER HAFTUNG (GmbH): The approximate German equivalent of the British private company.

GOING CONCERN: An accounting concept which assumes that an enterprise will continue in operational existence for the foreseeable future.

GOODWILL: The difference between the value of a company as a whole and the algebraic sum of the values of the assets and liabilities taken separately. Usually recorded only when purchased. The balance sheet figure therefore represents a past purchase price less amounts written off, not a current valuation.

GOODWILL ON CONSOLIDATION: The excess of the cost of shares in subsidiary companies over the book value of their net tangible assets at the date of acquisition. Can only appear in a *consolidated* balance sheet.

GOODWILL, PATENTS AND TRADE MARKS: Must be shown as separate item (but not necessarily as separate items) in published balance sheets together with method used to arrive at the amounts shown. *See also* under separate headings.

GROUP ACCOUNTS: Financial statements of a group of companies as distinct from the holding company only. The Companies Acts provide that they are submitted if a company has subsidiary companies and is not a wholly owned subsidiary of another company incorporated in Great Britain.

GUARANTEE, COMPANY LIMITED BY: A company the liability of whose members is limited to contributing a predetermined amount in the event of the company being wound up. Companies may be limited by guarantee or by shares, or be unlimited.

HARMONIZATION: The process of narrowing differences in accounting practices, especially among countries.

HISTORICAL COST: The traditional basis of valuation in published financial statements. Favoured because it is more objective and more easily verifiable by an auditor. SSAP 16 provides for the historical cost accounts to be either the main accounts or supplementary to current cost accounts. Adequate historical cost information must always be given.

HOLDING COMPANY: Company which controls another company, called its subsidiary. Balance sheet of holding company must show separately shares (including basis of valuation) and amounts owing to and owed by subsidiaries.

IMPUTATION SYSTEM: System of corporate taxation under which all or part of the tax paid on distributed profits by the company is credited to the shareholders, thus mitigating double taxation.

INCOME STATEMENT: American term for Profit and Loss Account (q.v.).

INCOME TAX: A tax on individuals not payable by companies. The basic rate of income tax varies; in 1980/81 it was 30 per cent.

INDUSTRY RATIO: An average ratio for an industry.

INFLATION ACCOUNTING: System of accounting which allows for changes in general and/or specific prices. *See also* Current Cost Accounting *and* Current Purchasing Power Accounting.

INITIAL ALLOWANCE: Allowance for tax purposes (currently 50 per cent) given in the first year of life of industrial buildings. Unlike an Investment Allowance (q.v.) it restricts the amount of the Writing-Down Allowances (q.v.) also given.

INSOLVENCY: An inability to pay debts as they fall due.

INSTITUTIONAL SHAREHOLDERS: Shareholders other than persons, industrial and commercial companies, the public sector and the overseas sector, i.e. financial institutions such as insurance companies and pension funds. Of increasing importance.

INTANGIBLE ASSETS: Assets such as goodwill, patents, trade marks and research and development expenditure to the extent that it is capitalized.

INTERIM DIVIDEND: *see* Dividend.

INTERIM REPORT: Report issued by a company to its shareholders during a financial year, e.g. quarterly, half-yearly.

INVENTORIES: American term for stock-in-trade.

INVESTMENT ALLOWANCE: Allowance for tax purposes formerly given in first year of life of some fixed assets. Unlike an Initial Allowance (q.v.) it did not restrict the amount of the Writing-Down Allowances (q.v.) also given. The total allowances granted were thus greater than the acquisition cost (less scrap value) of the asset.

INVESTMENTS: *see* Listed Investments *and* Unlisted Investments.

INVESTMENT TRUST: Not really a trust but a company whose object is investment in the securities of other companies. Compare Unit Trust.

IRREDEEMABLE DEBENTURE: A Debenture (q.v.) which will never have to be repaid.

ISSUED SHARE CAPITAL: The amount of the Authorized Share Capital (q.v.) which has been issued; the remainder is the unissued share capital. The amount of the issued capital must be disclosed in the published balance sheet. Not necessarily equal to called-up or paid-up share capital.

ISSUE EXPENSES: Expenses of making an issue of shares or debentures. Disclosed in balance sheet to extent that not written off.

ISSUE PRICE: The price at which a share or debenture is issued; not necessarily equal to the Par Value (q.v.).

LEASING: Entering into a long-term contract which allows the use of an asset in return for a periodic rental, but does not give ownership. Its effect is similar to financing the purchase of the asset by loan capital.

LEVERAGE: The American term for Gearing (q.v.).

LIABILITIES: Amounts owing by a company. The following must be disclosed in the published balance sheet:

1. aggregate amount of bank loans and overdrafts;

2. aggregate amount of other loans made to the company which are:

(i) not repayable by instalments and repayable after five years from balance sheet date, or

(ii) repayable by instalments any of which fall due for payment after five years from balance sheet date, together with details of repayment and rates of interest (if number of loans is large a general indication will suffice);

3. amounts due to subsidiary companies;

4. amounts due to other group members distinguishing between debentures and other indebtedness;

5. recommended dividend;

6. redeemed debentures which the company has the power to reissue;

7. any liability secured (otherwise than by operation of law) on the assets of the company (the assets need not be specified).

LIMITED LIABILITY COMPANY: A company the liability of whose members is limited by shares or by guarantee. If by shares, liability is limited to the amount taken up or agreed to be taken up; if by guarantee, to the amount undertaken to be contributed in the event of winding-up.

LIQUID ASSETS: *see* Quick Assets.

LISTED COMPANY: A public company listed (quoted) on a recognized stock exchange.

LISTED INVESTMENTS: Investments which are listed on a recognized stock exchange or on any reputable stock exchange outside Great Britain. Must be shown separately in the balance sheet.

LOAN CAPITAL: Funds acquired by non-short-term borrowing from sources other than the shareholders of the company.

LOANS RECEIVABLE: Must be shown in balance sheet if come under the following headings:

1. loans to employees (or trustees for employees) or salaried directors to enable them to purchase fully paid shares in the company or its holding company;

2. loans made during the year (whether repaid or not) by the company, a subsidiary, or by a third party secured or guaranteed by the company or subsidiary, to directors or officials of the company (except loans made in the ordinary course of business or loans not exceeding £2,000 made to employees).

LONG-TERM DEBT: Long-term sources of funds other than equity (share capital and reserves).

MAINSTREAM CORPORATION TAX: The difference between a company's total liability to corporation tax and advance corporation tax.

MARKET PRICE: The price at which a company's securities can be bought or sold on a stock exchange. Not necessarily equal to the Par Value or the Issue Price (qq.v.).

MATERIALITY: An accounting concept that requires disclosure only of data that is significant enough to be relevant to the needs of a potential user.

MAXIMUM BASIS: Method of calculating Earnings Per Share (q.v.) based on the assumption that a company distributes all its profits and is liable to pay advance corporation tax on them.

MEMORANDUM OF ASSOCIATION: Document which states:

1. the name of the company;

2. that the company is a public company (if such is the case);

3. the situation of the registered office;

4. the objects of the company;

5. that the liability of the members is limited (unless the company is an unlimited one);

6. the authorized share capital and how it is divided (or, in the case of a company limited by guarantee, the maximum amount to be contributed by members on winding-up);

7. details of the subscribers (the persons 'desirous of being formed into a company').

MERGER ACCOUNTING: A system of accounting which assumes the merger of two or more companies rather than the takeover of one by another.

MINORITY INTEREST: That part of a subsidiary company's shareholders' funds that is not held by the holding company. Usually shown as a separate item on the capital and liabilities side of a consolidated balance sheet.

MONETARY WORKING CAPITAL ADJUSTMENT (MWCA): An adjustment made in current cost accounting in order to take account of effect of increased prices on monetary working capital (bank balances + debtors − creditors).

NET BASIS: Method of calculating Earnings Per Share (q.v.) which takes account of both constant and variable components in the tax charge.

NET CURRENT ASSETS: Another name for Working Capital (q.v.).

NET PROFIT RATIO: Ratio of net profit to sales.

NET REALIZABLE VALUE: The amount for which an asset can be sold, net of the expenses of sale.

NET TANGIBLE ASSETS: Assets except for intangible assets *less* liabilities.

NET WORKING CAPITAL: Another name for Working Capital (q.v.).

NIL BASIS: Method of calculating Earnings Per Share (q.v.) which assumes a nil distribution of dividends.

NOMINAL SHARE CAPITAL: *see* Authorized Share Capital.

NON-VOTING SHARES: Shares with no voting rights. Non-voting ordinary shares are usually cheaper to buy than those carrying votes. Often called 'A' shares.

NO PAR VALUE SHARES: Shares with no nominal or par value. They are illegal in Britain.

NOTES TO THE ACCOUNTS: Notes attached to and explanatory of items in the financial statements. May be very detailed.

OBJECTIVITY: Accounting concept which stresses the need to establish rules for recording financial transactions and events which so far as possible do not depend upon the personal judgment of the recorder.

ORDINARY SHARES: Shares entitled to share in the profits after payment of debenture interest and preference dividends. Often referred to as the equity capital.

PAID-UP SHARE CAPITAL: The amount of the Called-Up Share Capital (q.v.) which has been paid up by the shareholders.

PARENT COMPANY: *see* Holding Company.

PAR VALUE: The face or nominal value of a share or debenture. Not necessarily equal to the Issue Price or the current Market Price (qq.v.). Dividend and interest percentages refer to the par value, Yields (q.v.) to the current market price.

PATENTS: Grants by the Crown to the authors of new inventions giving them the sole and exclusive right to use, exercise and sell their inventions and to secure the profits arising therefrom for a limited period.

POST BALANCE SHEET EVENTS: Events occurring after the date of the balance sheet. They are either 'adjusting events' (those providing additional evidence of conditions existing at the balance sheet date) or 'non-adjusting events'.

PRE-ACQUISITION PROFITS: The accumulated profits of a subsidiary company up to the date of its acquisition (take-over) by the holding company.

PREFERENCE SHARES: Shares which usually are entitled to a fixed rate of dividend before a dividend is paid on the ordinary shares and to priority of repayment if the company is wound up. Participating preference shares are also entitled to a further dividend if profits are available. If a preference dividend is not paid the arrears must be disclosed as a footnote to the balance sheet. Arrears can only arise if the shares are *cumulative* as distinct from *non-cumulative*.

PRELIMINARY EXPENSES: Expenses of forming a company. Disclosed as an asset in the balance sheet to extent that not written off.

PRICE—EARNINGS RATIO: The multiple of the last reported Earnings Per Share (q.v.) that the market is willing to pay per ordinary share. The reciprocal of the Earnings Yield (q.v.) multiplied by 100.

PRIOR CHARGES: Claims on a company's assets and profits that rank ahead of ordinary share capital.

PRIORITY PERCENTAGES: Method of calculating Gearing (q.v.) by computing the percentage of earnings that is required to service each category of loan and share capital.

PRIOR YEAR ADJUSTMENTS: Material adjustments applicable to prior years arising from changes in accounting policies or from the correction of fundamental errors.

PRIVATE COMPANY: A company which is not a Public Company (q.v.). Not permitted to issue shares or debentures to the public.

PROFIT: Revenues less expenses. Reported before and after extraordinary items and before and after tax.

PROFIT AND LOSS ACCOUNT: Gives details of a company's revenues, expenses and profit. Must by law give a 'true and fair view' of the profit or loss of the company for the financial year and disclose, *inter alia*:

1. provision for depreciation, renewals or diminution in value of fixed assets;

2. interest payable on the following loans (whether secured by debentures or not):
   i) bank loans and overdrafts,
   ii) loans repayable within five years by instalments,
   iii) loans not repayable by instalments but due for repayment within five years,
   iv) other loans;

3. taxation:
   i) amount and basis of the charge for U.K. corporation tax,
   ii) corporation tax relieved by double taxation agreements,
   iii) overseas taxation,
   iv) any special circumstances affecting taxation liability for the financial year or succeeding financial years;

4. amounts provided for redemption of share capital and redemption of loans;

5. transfers to and from reserves;

6. income from:

i) listed investments,

ii) unlisted investments;

7. rents (less outgoings) from land (if substantial);

8. charges for the hire of plant and machinery;

9. dividends paid and proposed;

10. charges or credits relating to prior years;

11. remuneration (including expenses) of the auditors;

12. amount and basis of turnover, except from banking and discounting (not required if company not part of a group and turnover does not exceed £1,000,000);

13. unusual, exceptional or non-recurring items and details of any change in the basis of accounting.

(*Note*: Above requirements include appropriations of profit. Thus published profit and loss account is really a profit and loss account proper plus a profit and loss appropriation account.)

PROFIT AND LOSS APPROPRIATION ACCOUNT: Continuation of profit and loss account proper giving details of profit appropriations, i.e. distribution as dividends and retention as reserves.

PROSPECTUS: Any notice, circular, advertisement or other invitation offering share or debentures to the public.

PROVISION: Defined by the Companies Acts as any amount written off or retained by way of providing for depreciation, renewals or diminution in the value of assets or providing for a known liability of which the amount cannot be determined with substantial accuracy. Examples: provision for depreciation, provision for doubtful debts. A charge against profit, not an appropriation of profit. Should not be confused with a Reserve (q.v.).

PROXY:

1. a person appointed to attend and vote at a company meeting on behalf of a shareholder;

2. the form, signed by the shareholder, which grants the above authority.

PRUDENCE: Accounting concept under which revenue and profits are not anticipated, but are recognized by inclusion in the profit and loss account only when realized in cash or other assets, the ultimate realization of which can be assessed with reasonable certainty. Provision is made for all known liabilities whether the amount of these is known with certainty or is a best estimate in the light of the information available.

PUBLIC COMPANY: A company whose Memorandum of Association (q.v.) states that it is a public company, whose name ends with the words 'public limited company' (plc; ccc for Welsh companies) and which has a minimum authorized and allotted share capital at least one quarter paid up.

QUICK ASSETS: Current assets *less* stock-in-trade.

QUICK RATIO: The relationship between quick assets and current liabilities. Also known as liquid ratio, or the acid test. A measure of liquidity.

RECOVERABLE AMOUNT: The greater of the Net Realizable Value (q.v.) of an asset and the amount recoverable from its further use.

REDEEMABLE PREFERENCE SHARES: Preference shares which must or may be redeemed at the option of the company or (very rarely) the shareholder. The balance sheet must disclose the earliest and latest dates on which the company has power to redeem, whether at the option of the company or in any event, and also the amount of any premium on redemption.

REDEMPTION YIELD: A Yield (q.v.) which takes into account not only the annual interest receivable but also the redemption value of a security.

REDUCING BALANCE DEPRECIATION: Method of depreciation in which the periodic amount written off decreases over the life of the asset. A fixed percentage is applied to a declining written-down value.

REGISTERED OFFICE: The official address of a company. The Memorandum of Association (q.v.) must state whether it is in England and Wales, Wales, or Scotland.

REGISTRAR OF COMPANIES: Government officer with whom annual reports (including financial statements) and other documents must be filed; in Cardiff for companies registered in England and Wales, in Edinburgh for companies registered in Scotland.

REPLACEMENT COST: The amount payable for an asset at the current time.

RESEARCH AND DEVELOPMENT EXPENDITURE: Includes expenditure on pure research, applied research and development. Only the last is in some circumstances treated as an asset.

RESERVE: Reserves arise either from the retention of profits or from events such as the issue of shares at a premium or the revaluation of assets. Must not include Provisions (q.v.) unless the directors consider the latter are excessive. Not a charge against profits; not necessarily represented by cash on the other side of the balance sheet. Movements in reserves during the financial year must be disclosed.

RESERVE FUND: A Reserve (q.v.) which is represented by specially earmarked cash or investments on the other side of the balance sheet.

RETAINED PROFITS: Profits not distributed to shareholders but re-invested in the company. Their cost is less than a new issue of shares, because of the issue costs of the latter.

RETURN ON INVESTMENT: Ratio of profit (usually before interest and tax) to net tangible assets. A measure of profitability.

REVALUATION: The writing-up of an asset to its current market value.

REVERSE YIELD GAP: A description of the fact that since August 1959 the average yield on government bonds has been greater than the average dividend yield on the ordinary shares of companies, despite the greater (monetary) security of the former.

RIGHTS ISSUE: An issue of shares in which the existing shareholders have a right to subscribe for the new shares at a stated price. The right can be sold if the shareholder does not wish to subscribe.

RISK: Of two kinds: Systematic (or market) risk and Specific (or non-market) risk (qq.v.).

SALE-AND-LEASEBACK: Raising cash by selling an asset and then leasing it back in a long-term contract. *See also* Leasing.

SCRAP VALUE: The amount at which a fixed asset is expected to be sold at the end of its estimated economic life.

SCRIP ISSUE: *see* Bonus Shares.

SECOND SCHEDULE, COMPANIES ACT 1967: Sets out in detail what must, subject to the overriding obligation to show a true and fair view, be disclosed in the published financial statements of companies.

SECURITIES AND EXCHANGE COMMISSION (SEC): American federal body concerned with the operations of corporations (i.e. companies) and issues of and dealings in their securities. It has the right, which it has largely delegated to the Financial Accounting Standards Board, to establish accounting principles.

SECURITY: Two meanings:

1. a generic name for stocks, share, debentures, etc.;
2. the backing for a loan.

SHARE CAPITAL: Unless limited by guarantee, a company registered under the Companies Acts must have a share capital divided into shares of a fixed amount. The ownership of a share gives the shareholder a proportionate ownership of the company. The share capital is stated in the balance sheet at its par (nominal) value.

SHAREHOLDER: Member of a company whose part ownership of (share in) the company is evidenced by a share certificate.

SHAREHOLDERS' FUNDS: The proprietorship section of a company balance sheet. Includes the share capital and the reserves.

SHARE OPTIONS: The right to buy or sell shares within a stated period.

SHARE PREMIUM: Results from issuing shares at a price higher than their par value. Must be disclosed in the balance sheet as a Reserve (q.v.). Cannot be used to pay dividends but can be used to make an issue of Bonus Shares (q.v.).

SOCIÉTÉ ANONYME (SA): The approximate French equivalent of a British public company.

SOCIÉTÉ À RESPONSABILITÉ LIMITÉE (SARL): The approximate French equivalent of a British private company.

SOURCE AND APPLICATION OF FUNDS, STATEMENT OF: A statement showing the sources of funds (e.g. new issue of shares or debentures, retained profits) and the uses of funds (e.g. purchase of new fixed assets, increase in working capital) of a company over a period.

SPECIFIC RISK: Risk arising from factors specific to a company and not from the market generally.

STATEMENTS OF STANDARD ACCOUNTING PRACTICE (SSAPS): Statements of methods of accounting approved by the Councils of the major professional accountancy bodies. They apply to all financial statements intended to give a true and fair view.

STOCK APPRECIATION RELIEF: A relief from corporation tax for that part of the increase in the money value of stock-in-trade which is due to increased prices and not increased volume.

STOCKBROKER: A member of a stock exchange who deals with the public.

STOCK DIVIDEND: *see* Bonus Shares.

STOCK EXCHANGE: A market where shares, debentures, government securities, etc. are bought and sold. The London Stock Exchange is by far the largest in Britain; it is federated with the provincial exchanges.

STOCKS AND WORK IN PROGRESS: Comprises goods or other assets purchased for resale; consumable stores; raw materials and components; products and services in intermediate stages of completion; and finished goods. Valued at the lower of cost (historical cost under historical cost accounting; replacement cost under current cost accounting) or net realizable value.

STOCK TURNOVER: Ratio of sales (sometimes, cost of sales) to stock-in-trade.

STRAIGHT-LINE DEPRECIATION: Obtained by dividing the cost less estimated scrap value of an asset by its estimated economic life.

SUBDIVISION OF SHARE CAPITAL: Splitting of shares into smaller units (e.g. splitting one £1 share into two of £0.50).

SUBSIDIARY: Company controlled by another company called its holding company. A company is a subsidiary of another company if that other company:

1. is a member of it; and
2. controls the composition of its board of directors; or
3. holds more than half the nominal value of its Equity Share Capital (q.v.).

The following information *inter alia* about subsidiaries must be disclosed:

1. name of each subsidiary and country of incorporation if other than Great Britain (if incorporated in G.B. country of registration – England, Wales or Scotland – unless holding company registered in same country);

2. proportion of nominal value of each class of the issued share capital of each subsidiary which is held by the holding company (or its nominees) or by a subsidiary company (or its nominees);

3. name and (if known) country of incorporation of the ultimate holding company of a subsidiary company.

Note: (i) 1 and 2 apply also to share investments when a company holds more than 5 per cent of nominal amount of any class of shares comprised in the equity share capital of a body corporate or where the share interest represents more than 5 per cent of the assets of the company holding the shares.

(ii) Companies incorporated in or carrying on business abroad may be excluded from requirements 1, 2 and 3 with the agreement of the Department of Trade.

SYSTEMATIC (MARKET) RISK: Risk arising from the market, not from specific factors applicable to a company. Quantified as the *beta* of a company's ordinary shares.

TABLE A: A model set of Articles of Association (q.v.) which can be adopted by a company in full or in a modified form.

TAKE-OVER BID: An offer to purchase the share capital of a company.

TANGIBLE ASSETS: Assets such as land and buildings, plant and machinery and fixtures and fittings.

TAXABLE INCOME: Income liable to tax. Not usually equal to the profit reported in a company's financial statements.

TAX CREDIT: A credit received by shareholders at the same time as a dividend. Its amount is based on the basic rate of income tax. It can be set off against the liability to income tax on the dividend plus tax credit.

TIMES INTEREST EARNED: The number of times that a company's interest is covered or earned by its profit before interest and tax.

TRADE CREDIT: Short-term source of funds resulting from credit granted by suppliers of goods bought.

TRADE MARK: A distinctive identification, protected by law, of a manufactured product or of a service.

TRADING ON THE EQUITY: American expression describing the process of using fixed-interest sources of capital to boost the return on the equity (ordinary shares).

TRUE AND FAIR VIEW: By law both the balance sheet and the profit and loss account must give a 'true and fair view'. The phrase is undefined but depends upon both the application of accounting standards and the exercise of judgment. The requirement of a true and fair view overrides the specific disclosure provisions of the Companies Acts.

TURNOVER: Sales. The profit and loss account must disclose the amount and basis of turnover for the financial year. The directors' report must disclose group turnover and profit (or loss) before tax divided among classes of business that differ substantially. Shown net of value added tax. (Exceptions: banking and discounting business and any company which is not part of a group and whose turnover does not exceed £1,000,000.)

ULTRA VIRES: Latin for 'beyond the powers'. Especially applied to acts of a company not authorized by the objects clause of its memorandum of association.

UNDISTRIBUTABLE RESERVES: The aggregate of a company's share premium account; capital redemption reserve fund; accumulated unrealized profits, so far as not previously capitalized, *less* accumulated, unrealized losses, so far as not previously written off in a reduction or reorganization of capital; and other reserves the company is prohibited from distributing.

UNIT TRUST: Undertaking formed to invest in securities (mainly ordinary shares) under the terms of a trust deed. Not a company. Compare Investment Trust.

UNLIMITED COMPANY: A Company (q.v.) the liability of whose members is limited neither by shares nor by guarantee.

UNLISTED INVESTMENTS: Investments which are not listed on a recognized British stock exchange or on any reputable stock exchange outside Great Britain. If they consist of equity of other companies directors must give either an estimate of their value or information about income received, profits, etc.

UNSECURED LOAN: Money borrowed by a company without the giving of security.

VALUE ADDED, STATEMENT OF: A statement showing for a period the wealth created (value added) by the operations of an enterprise and how the wealth has been distributed among employees, government, providers of capital and replacement and expansion.

VALUE ADDED TAX (VAT): A tax based on the value added as goods pass from supplier of raw materials, to manufacturer, to wholesaler, to retailer, to consumer. Tax receivable can be set off against tax payable. Turnover is shown net of VAT in published profit and loss accounts.

VALUE TO THE BUSINESS: The deprival value of an asset, i.e. the lower of its current replacement cost and Recoverable Amount (q.v.). The basis of valuation in current cost accounting.

VARIABLE OVERHEADS: Overheads which vary proportionately with manufacturing activity.

WINDOW-DRESSING: The manipulation of figures in financial statements so as to produce a desired ratio on the balance sheet date.

WORKING CAPITAL: Current assets *less* current liabilities.

WORK-IN-PROGRESS: Partly completed manufactured goods.

WRITING-DOWN ALLOWANCE: The annual amount deductible for tax purposes on motor vehicles (currently 25 per cent on a reducing balance basis) and on industrial buildings (currently 4 per cent on a straight-line basis).

WRITTEN-DOWN VALUE: The value of an asset in the books of a company or for tax purposes after depreciation has been written off.

YIELD: The rate of return relating cash invested to cash received (or expected to be received).

Appendix C *British Vita Report and Accounts 1979*

Contents

Results at a Glance

£000	**1979**	1978
Turnover	**73,296**	49,874
Trading profit	**6,875**	4,482
Share of profit of associated companies	**3,129**	2,793
Profit before tax:		
United Kingdom and Europe	**4,593**	3,009
International	**4,335**	3,823
	8,928	6,832
Profit attributable to shareholders	**6,762**	4,859
Average capital employed	**28,824**	22,780
Return on capital employed	**34·7%**	31·9%
Earnings per share	**34·1p**	24·8p
Dividend per share	**5·0p**	2·23p
Assets per share	**123p**	99p

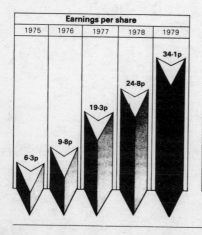

Earnings per share

1975	1976	1977	1978	1979
6·3p	9·8p	19·3p	24·8p	34·1p

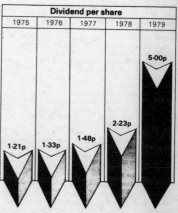

Dividend per share

1975	1976	1977	1978	1979
1·21p	1·33p	1·48p	2·23p	5·00p

Chairman's Review

The year

As a result of the dedicated work of the executive directors, the management and all personnel in our companies throughout the world, I can report a record result for 1979.

The pre-tax profit of £8·93m includes a full year's profits of Caligen Foam and Foam Components and, for part of the year, profits of Libeltex and Portways, both fibre processors acquired during the year. The full potential of these acquisitions has yet to be realised.

Libeltex and Portways were selected for their management capabilities, their technology and standing in the trade. Both form part of the Group's policy to establish fibre processing as a major product line based on the Group's technology and complementary to its present markets. This policy has been achieved in the UK and Europe and now fibre processing is being introduced into certain of our international operations.

Whilst the international operations achieved a 13% increase in profit, the earnings of the UK and European operations, assisted by recent acquisitions, grew by 53%. The Group has therefore further improved the quality of its earnings with the proportion of the results generated from its UK and European operations increasing to over half of the total profit. The cash flow so generated, enhanced by improved dividend remittances from overseas, has reinforced the Group's UK position, one result being the release of security on all the Group's UK bank borrowings.

For the second year the Report and Accounts include Current Cost Accounts showing the Group's profit and assets employed after adjusting for the effects of inflation. Management, of course, have to react to inflation on a day to day basis by off-setting the rising prices of our major raw materials and increased overhead costs either by increased efficiency or adjustment to selling prices. In the present times of high inflation levels, considerable management effort and determination is required to maintain the right degree of profitability.

In 1979 the Group acquired £5·3m fixed assets excluding the new investments in subsidiaries. The major expenditure was to update the Group's plant and equipment particularly in the UK and Europe, the most important project being the new foam plant at Middleton. This installation, based on today's technology and engineering, besides achieving improved quality and efficiency, is well advanced in ensuring better protection for the health and safety of personnel and for the environment generally.

It is Group policy to improve wherever possible the health and safety conditions for its personnel and this is a major consideration in the installation of all new plant.

Internationally our subsidiary companies all achieved good results, especially in the second half of the year although some element of that profit arose from non-recurring contracts. Most of our associated companies made good progress during the year and production facilities have been improved in many areas. In Nigeria manufacturing commenced at a new plant in Sapele whilst at Jos a new factory is nearing completion. Vitafoam Australia opened a new plant at Brisbane and in Egypt a large modern foaming plant in a new factory was commissioned in October.

During the year personnel from our overseas operations have been to the UK to attend courses at business schools and production and management development courses at our own plants. Meanwhile the interchange of technology throughout the Group has assisted the introduction of new products to several areas.

The future

Since the end of our financial year we have acquired Vita-tex, a leading textile processor specialising in the printing, dyeing, laminating and finishing of textiles for a variety of uses. The products made and technology employed by Vita-tex enable it to serve customers in a wide range of markets in which the Group is already a major supplier. The Group's overseas interests provide opportunities for the development of new outlets for Vita-tex products and technology.

The Group, through Vitafoam and then British Vita, has ended the first three decades of its existence and is now entering a new decade with a broad product range and its personnel supported by technology and engineering. It is the intention of the Boards of British Vita, its subsidiaries and associates to continue our growth both at home and overseas. We cannot expect the economic climate to be always in our favour during the whole of the next decade but there will be opportunities to be grasped to achieve the growth we require. Your Board intends that progress be secured by extending the scope of the Group's technology into allied areas, by extending the range of products supplied into the markets we serve, and by seeking new markets for our products. The Group's engineering skills will be deployed in designing safe and efficient plant and equipment which will maintain the appropriate balance between production costs and competitiveness and hence preserve profitability.

Once again the new financial year has commenced with a major strike in a basic industry. In addition some parts of British industry are also suffering a downturn in trade due to destocking taking place in the face of record interest rates and low consumer demand. As a result of these conditions, which are affecting particularly consumer durables, your Company's operations serving those markets have had a difficult start to the year. However, the Group enjoys a wide spread of operations and your Board and management are determined that every effort will be made to minimise the effects of these outside circumstances.

Dividends

The abolition of dividend control enabled the Board to declare an interim dividend more commensurate with the performance of the Company. As indicated in my interim statement the proposed final dividend reflects this policy.

Personnel

I am pleased that despite the restrictive taxation on share option schemes introduced in 1974 many of our personnel will be benefiting this year from options granted under our schemes. In particular those of our personnel who were granted options under the Own As You Earn scheme in February 1975, at an option price of 25p per share, can now exercise these options, which attract bonus issues made during the option period, and so benefit from the improvement in the Group which they have helped to achieve.

The Company continues to give priority to reviewing pensions and related benefits for its employees, pensioners and their dependants.

The Company's UK pension schemes, operated through trustees, are funded at rates recommended by actuaries. The trustees are advised by investment managers and the schemes actuarially valued every two years; the 1979 actuarial valuation showed all the schemes to be in surplus. In addition to the well-established schemes in the UK, several of our overseas subsidiaries and associates have, or are in the process of introducing, their own schemes.

In conclusion I wish to express my personal thanks to all the Group's personnel throughout the world for their efforts during the 1970's and to welcome again those joining the Group in the past two years. In February this year I had the pleasure of welcoming to the Board Norman M. Grimshaw, General Manager of the Consumer Products Division and son of the late Chairman. I recommend him for re-election at the Annual General Meeting.

14 March 1980

Directors

Chairman	F. A. Parker, FCA, MBIM
Deputy Chairman and Chief Executive	R. McGee, LPRI
Deputy Chairman	H. Houghton (Non-executive)
Directors	G. Blunt, MBIM
	F. J. Eaton, APRI
	N. M. Grimshaw
	D. R. Hine, BSc, CEng, MIChemE, AMCT
	L. D. Lawton, BA, FRSA
	J. H. Ogden (Non-executive)
	T. Richardson, FIPM
	R. H. Sellers, BSc(Econ), FCA, DpBA
Director and Secretary	W. E. Holt, LLB
Registered Office	Soudan Street, Middleton, Manchester M24 2DB
	(Registered in England No 871669)
Auditors	C. Connelly,
	Chartered Accountants,
	Market Street, Huddersfield HD1 2EX
Principal Bankers	National Westminster Bank Limited
Registrars and Transfer Office	National Westminster Bank Limited,
	Registrars Department, Bristol BS99 7NH

Notice of Meeting

NOTICE IS HEREBY GIVEN that the Fourteenth Annual General Meeting of British Vita Company Limited will be held at the Midway Hotel, Castleton, Rochdale on Wednesday, 16 April 1980 at 12.00 noon for the following purposes:

1 To receive and consider the Accounts and the Reports of the directors and auditors for the year ended 31 December 1979.

2 To confirm the dividends paid and to declare a final dividend on the Ordinary shares for the year ended 31 December 1979.

3 To re-elect directors:
Mr J. H. Ogden retires by rotation and will be proposed for re-election in accordance with Article 109.
Mr N. M. Grimshaw who has been appointed by the Board since the last Annual General Meeting will be proposed for re-election in accordance with Article 92.

4 To re-appoint Messrs C. Connelly as auditors of the Company.

5 To authorise the directors to fix the remuneration of the auditors.

6 To transact any other ordinary business of the Company.

Any member of the Company entitled to attend and vote is entitled to appoint one or more proxies (whether members or not) to attend and, on a poll, vote instead of him. A form of proxy and the power of attorney or other authority (if any) under which it is signed or a notarially certified copy of that power or authority must be deposited at the Registered Office of the Company, Soudan Street, Middleton, Manchester M24 2DB not less than 24 hours before the time for holding the meeting.
A form of proxy is included as page 31 of the Report and Accounts.

Dated 25 March 1980
By Order of the Board
W. E. Holt, *Secretary*
Soudan Street, Middleton,
Manchester M24 2DB

Copies of the Accounts and the Report of the directors are sent to the Preference shareholders, Debenture stockholders and Loan noteholders in accordance with Section 158 of the Companies Act 1948. However, they are neither entitled to attend nor vote at the above meeting unless they are holders also of Ordinary shares.
Copies of contracts of service (unless expiring or determinable by the employing company without payment of compensation within one year) between the Company's directors and the Company or a subsidiary will be available for inspection at the Registered Office of the Company on any weekday (Saturdays and public holidays excepted) during normal business hours and for a period of fifteen minutes prior to and during the meeting.

Group Operations

Group structure

By the late 1970's, the structure of the Group had significantly changed through a process of rationalisation in certain existing product areas, organic growth in key areas and selective acquisitions. The management organisation was strengthened by the development of autonomous business units, operating within general Group guidelines but with individual profit responsibility vested in the respective Business Managers. This organisation, headed by the Executive Control Group, each member having specific business responsibilities, provides for a unified approach in relation to the Group's corporate objectives whilst promoting entrepreneurial activity in individual businesses.

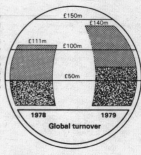

Global turnover

Turnover

Turnover of British Vita Company Limited and its subsidiaries in 1979 was £73·3m, an increase of 136% in the last five years. In the same period total turnover of associated companies increased from £20m to £67m bringing Global turnover of the Group to £140m in 1979.

British Vita & subsidiaries

Associated companies

UK and Europe operations

The Group principally manufactures plastic and rubber products; the range of manufacturing units and products in the UK and European markets is indicated on the inside front cover. The relative size of individual product and market groupings based on 1979 turnover in UK and Europe is:

By product	£m	By market	%
Cellular foams	28	Furniture	29
Industrial rubber compounds and components	15	General industry	24
		Household textiles and consumer	19
Fibre and fabric processing	10	Transportation	13
Consumer	7	Bedding	6
Service	6	Other	9
	66		100

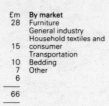

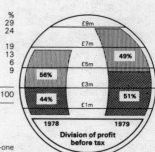

Division of profit before tax

UK & Europe

International

International operations

British Vita has substantial international interests in twenty-one countries throughout Africa, Australasia, Canada, the Caribbean and the Far East, principally through associated companies most of which are engaged in the manufacture of foam but several also having significant interests in related consumer and furniture products. In addition there are four subsidiaries in Africa whose products include furniture, foam and coated fabrics.

Vita-tex Limited

Vita-tex Limited joined the British Vita Group on 5 February 1980 and on the same date the sale of assets upon which the Offer was conditional was completed.

Operations

The company, whose main operations are at Slough, has approximately 250 employees and annual sales currently in excess of £11m. It has evolved from being a manufacturer of traditional warp knitted fabrics to its present position as a leading textile processor specialising in the printing, dyeing, laminating and finishing of textiles. The acquisition complements and increases the Group's involvement in the transportation, household textile and consumer markets.

1979 results

In the twelve months to 31 December 1979, Vita-tex profit before tax, based on management accounts and excluding the contribution from assets which have been sold since that date, was £1,150,000.

In order to give shareholders an indication of the Group's assets and capital employed following the acquisition, the unaudited statement below sets out the Group balance sheet consolidating the purchase of Vita-tex. The statement is based on the Group balance sheet at 31 December 1979 and the unaudited Vita-tex balance sheet as at that date adjusted for the effects of the sale of assets referred to in the preceding paragraph.

£000

Assets employed

Fixed assets	18,330
Associated companies	8,752
Deferred assets	728
	27,810
Net current assets	9,069
	36,879

Capital employed

Issued share capital	5,280
Reserves	19,687
	24,967
Minority interests in subsidiaries	265
Loans	9,368
Long term creditors	2,279
	36,879

Directors' Report

Profit and dividends

The profit attributable to shareholders for the year ended 31 December 1979 is £6,762,000. After provision for dividends of £1,023,000 the profit retained in the Group for the year is £5,739,000 of which £2,805,000 is retained in the Company.

An interim dividend of 2·4p per Ordinary share was paid on 2 November 1979. The directors now propose a final dividend of 2·6p per Ordinary share payable on 6 May 1980 to shareholders on the Register on 8 April 1980.

The total Ordinary dividend for the year is 5p per share, an increase of 125% over the corresponding total for 1978 (adjusted for the 1979 capitalisation issue) of 2·23p per share.

Principal activities

The Group is principally concerned with the manufacture of cellular foams, synthetic fibre fillings, rubber and plastic compounds, precision rubber mouldings and fabrications, coated fabrics, adhesives and a range of consumer products. Service activities include haulage contracting, merchanting and property management.

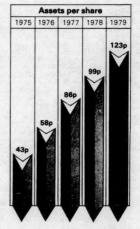

Assets per share

	1975	1976	1977	1978	1979
	43p	58p	86p	99p	123p

Analysis of turnover and trading profit
(excluding associated companies)

	Turnover		Trading profit	
£000	**1979**	1978	**1979**	1978
Manufacturing				
UK	**55,478**	40,441	**4,588**	2,803
Europe	**7,287**	260	**388**	13
Africa	**7,168**	6,424	**1,630**	1,346
	69,933	47,125	**6,606**	4,162
Service				
UK	**3,363**	2,749	**269**	320
	73,296	49,874	**6,875**	4,482

Export turnover for the year included in the UK figures above amounted to £3,392,000 (£2,783,000)

Subsidiary companies

With effect from 1 January 1979, the Company acquired the whole of the issued share capital of Foam Components Limited, a London based specialised converter of foam for £235,000 payable in cash.

On 4 July 1979 the acquisition was completed of the Belgian company Libeltex NV, a major European manufacturer of bonded fibre waddings, for a cash consideration of £1,308,000. Attributable net tangible assets at completion were £1,084,000 including freehold land and buildings at valuation on an existing use basis by Richard Ellis SA of Brussels.

Portways Limited, a manufacturer of fibre fillings and related consumer products based at Tipton, West Midlands, was acquired with effect from 28 October 1979. The cash consideration was £1,171,000 and net tangible assets at that date were £696,000, based on accounts prepared as at 27 October 1979.

A summary of the net tangible assets acquired in the above transactions is given on page 28. The acquired companies' balance sheets as at 31 December 1979, together with the related goodwill on acquisition totalling £870,000 which has been deducted from Group reserves, are consolidated in the Group balance sheet on page 17. In accordance with Group accounting policies only the results from the respective acquisition dates have been brought into the Group profit and loss account on page 16 and include turnover of £4,740,000 and profit before tax of £280,000.

During the year Vita Polymers Europe BV was incorporated. It holds certain of the Group's interests in Africa and, through its newly incorporated subsidiary Vitafoam Europe BV, the Group's interests in Continental Europe.

During 1979, Furniture Corporation of Zambia Limited and Vitafoam Zambia Limited issued, at par, ordinary shares to A. Z. Mokola, managing director of both companies, as a consequence of which his interest in the ordinary share capital of each company has increased from 3% to 4.98%.

During the year the Group determined to effect 25% local participation in Vitafoam Kenya Limited, pursuant to one of the terms of an agreement with the Kenyan Government, by issuing shares in that company to the Kenyan executive directors and two senior executives. Accordingly in the profit and loss account, 10% of the profits of Vitafoam Kenya for the first nine months of the year and 25% of the profits for the last quarter have been attributed to minority shareholders. The shares, which have been issued at par, partly paid, were allotted in February 1980.

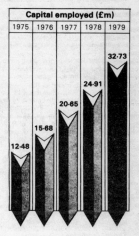

Capital employed (£m)

1975	1976	1977	1978	1979
12·48	15·68	20·65	24·91	32·73

Associated companies

During the year the issued share capital of Taki-Vita SAE was increased from E£1·1m to E£2·0m. The Group's proportion of the increased capital (E£360,000) was mainly financed from loans already made to that company.

Vitafoam Australia Pty Limited has recently established a joint venture company in Papua New Guinea to manufacture foam products. In addition Vitafoam Australia has acquired, for A$1,752,000 cash consideration, 11% of the issued share capital of Clark Rubber Limited, an Australian public company and a major customer. Clark Rubber holds 20% of the issued share capital of Vitafoam Australia.

Fixed assets

Details of the fixed assets are given on page 20. Excluding the investments in subsidiary companies noted above, the Group expended £5,284,000 on fixed assets during the year.

Finance

During the year £3,158,000 was paid in respect of consideration for acquisitions. Due to the strength of sterling in mid year, the opportunity was taken to effect early repayment of certain foreign currency loans in the sterling equivalent of £850,000 and scheduled repayments of medium term loans in the year were also made totalling £431,000.

The source and application of funds statement on page 28 shows the funds generated from operations and how the additional funding required was financed. Increase in loans includes new medium term loans totalling £2,406,000.

Total capital employed in the Group at 31 December 1979 had increased to £32,734,000 and assets per share to 123p.

On 5 February 1980 the Company's Offer for all the then issued share capital of Vita-tex Limited became unconditional in all respects. As at that date acceptances had been received in respect of 96·05% of the share capital of Vita-tex and the balance of the capital is being acquired.

Pursuant to the terms of the Offer there will ultimately be allotted approximately 1,008,000 new British Vita Ordinary shares, £2,050,000 Guaranteed Floating Rate Unsecured Loan Notes 1985 and £807,000 cash.

It was a condition of the Offer that Vita-tex sell to three of the Vita-tex directors and their associate certain assets not germane to Vita-tex's mainstream activities. As a consequence of that condition being satisfied and completion of the sale of other freehold property, in February Vita-tex received £898,800 cash and in addition was released from certain liabilities including a bank loan of £300,000.

Directors
The directors currently holding office are listed on page 4. Mr D. R. Hine and Mr W. E. Holt were appointed directors on 4 January 1979. Mr J. H. Ogden retires by rotation at the Annual General Meeting and being eligible offers himself for re-election.

On 7 February 1980 Mr N. M. Grimshaw was elected a director and in accordance with Article 92 offers himself for re-election at the Annual General Meeting.

Directors and other interests
The interests of the directors in the share capital of the Company as at 31 December 1979 are shown below. Also shown are the interests of Mr N. M. Grimshaw as at 7 February 1980, the date of his appointment to the Board.

Name	Class of shares	31 December 1979			31 December 1978 (or at date of appointment if later)		
		Beneficial	As trustee	Options†	Beneficial	As trustee	Options†
F. A. Parker*	Ordinary	1,497,397	3,154,747	—	1,265,958	3,319,624	—
	Preference	—	21,950		—	21,950	
R. McGee	Ordinary	177,744	773,526	51,648	140,320	727,939	54,600
G. Blunt	Ordinary	127,559	773,526	37,248	100,000	727,939	42,600
F. J. Eaton	Ordinary	49,720	773,526	28,530	39,434	727,939	29,280
D. R. Hine	Ordinary	13,423	—	14,400	8,786	—	14,400
W. E. Holt	Ordinary	14,347	—	28,080	14,347	—	28,200
H. Houghton*	Ordinary	1,531	773,526	—	1,276	727,939	—
L. D. Lawton*	Ordinary	136,230	773,526	35,022	109,826	727,939	38,400
J. H. Ogden*	Ordinary	30,000	3,406,019	—	30,000	3,571,018	—
	Preference	—	45,850	—		47,450	—
T. Richardson	Ordinary	66,393	773,526	35,610	55,128	727,939	39,000
R. H. Sellers	Ordinary	23,000	773,526	28,608	18,000	727,939	28,200
N. M. Grimshaw	Ordinary	444,960	1,958,719	15,408			

†After adjusting for capitalisation issues to relevant year end.
*Not eligible to participate in the Company's share option schemes.

The only change in the interests of the directors between 31 December 1979 and 25 February 1980 or if later the date of their appointment and 25 February 1980 has been the sale of 10,000 Ordinary shares by Mr L. D. Lawton on 8 January 1980 at a price of 127·5p per share.

No director has any interest in the Company's debentures nor any significant interest in any contract or arrangement entered into by the Company or its subsidiaries.

So far as the directors are aware no other person or group of persons, other than a director and Nutraco Nominees Limited (holding 1,204,622 shares representing 5·8%) held an interest comprising 5% or more in the issued share capital of the Company as at 25 February 1980.

Employee share options

The Company's share option schemes were adopted in 1974 and options first offered in 1975. Under the 1977 Supplementary Rules of the schemes, option holders, on exercise of their options over shares within the original grants, are issued with further shares, fully paid out of a special reserve, to reflect the capitalisation issues to Ordinary shareholders made between the respective dates of grant and exercise of the original options.

Since 1975 the Company has effected three capitalisation issues: April 1977–1:1, April 1978–1:5 and April 1979–1:5.

Options under the Own As You Earn scheme are exercisable after the fifth anniversary of the date of grant. Options under the Executive and International schemes are exercisable between the third and seventh anniversaries of the date of grant.

The total of unissued Ordinary shares appropriated by the Company to its share option schemes was 1,499,618 at 31 December 1979 and the table below sets out details of the appropriation:

	Date of grant	Option share price	Option shares	Total shares appropriated for: existing options	future grant
Own As You Earn scheme	Feb 1975	25·0p	29,000	83,520	
	Feb 1976	49·5p	26,125	75,240	
	Jan 1977	80·1p	54,250	156,240	
	Apr 1978	72·0p	65,850	94,824	
	Apr 1979	130·5p	78,430	94,116	
				503,940	243,060
Executive scheme	Feb 1975	42·0p	55,300	159,264	
	Feb 1976	60·0p	51,600	148,608	
	Jan 1977	95·0p	75,700	218,016	
	Mar 1978	80·0p	37,900	54,576	
	Dec 1978	117·0p	32,000	38,400	
	Mar 1979	145·0p	8,700	10,440	
				629,304	43,154 *
International scheme	Apr 1978	82·0p	46,100	66,384	
	Apr 1978	67·0p	3,600	4,320	
	Jun 1978	88·0p	2,880	3,456	
	Oct 1979	145·0p	6,000	6,000	
				80,160	
				1,213,404	286,214

*Available for grant under Executive and International schemes. Since 31 December 1979 options over 9,000 shares have been granted under the Executive scheme at 162p per share.

Ordinary share capital

During the year 3,303,727 shares were issued in accordance with the resolution authorising the capitalisation issue passed on 11 April 1979. In addition options were exercised by participants in the share option schemes resulting in the issue of 107,877 shares.

At 25 February 1980 20,863,201 shares were in issue including 980,129 shares allotted pursuant to the Offer for Vita-tex and 360 shares issued under the OAYE scheme since 31 December 1979.

Close company provisions

The close company provisions of the Income and Corporation Taxes Act 1970, as subsequently amended, do not apply to the Company. There has been no change in this respect since the end of the financial year.

Personnel

The average number of persons employed by the Group in the United Kingdom each week during the year was 2,842 and the aggregate gross remuneration paid to them for the year was £12,093,000. Overseas there were 4,045 personnel employed in the Group's subsidiary and associated companies.

The Group continues to maintain its policy of concern for the health, safety and welfare of its employees both in the UK and overseas.

Donations

Charitable donations made by the Group during the year amounted to £3,200. £550 was paid to the Economic League.

Auditors

In accordance with S.14 of the Companies Act 1976 a resolution proposing the re-appointment of Messrs C. Connelly as auditors of the Company will be put to the Annual General Meeting.

By Order of the Board
W. E. Holt
Secretary

14 March 1980

British Vita Group 1975-1979

£000	1975	1976	1977	1978	**1979**
Turnover and profit					
Turnover (excluding associated companies)	31,039	37,907	44,042	49,874	**73,296**
Trading profit	488	1,409	3,122	4,482	**6,875**
Share of profit of associated companies	2,299	3,084	3,561	2,793	**3,129**
Interest	(456)	(472)	(504)	(443)	**(1,076)**
Profit before tax	2,331	4,021	6,179	6,832	**8,928**
Tax	(1,103)†	(2,100)	(2,400)	(1,923)	**(2,102)**
Minority interests	—	—	—	(20)	**(64)**
Extraordinary items and Preference dividend	(210)	(392)	111	(32)	**(2)**
Profit attributable to Ordinary shareholders	1,018	1,529	3,890	4,857	**6,760**
Ordinary dividend: payable	(236)	(260)	(290)	(440)	**(1,021)**
interim waived	17	19	20	—	**—**
Profit retained	799	1,288	3,620	4,417	**5,739**
Capital employed					
Fixed assets	6,476	6,696	8,408	11,406	**17,012**
Associated companies and deferred assets	2,284	5,166	7,538	7,814	**9,343**
Net current assets	3,717	3,817	4,700	5,694	**6,379**
	12,477	15,679	20,646	24,914	**32,734**
Financed by					
Shareholders' funds	8,611	12,141	16,982	19,591	**24,458**
External sources	3,866†	3,538	3,664	5,323	**8,276**
	12,477	15,679	20,646	24,914	**32,734**
Ratios					
Trading profit as a percentage of turnover	1·6%	3·7%	7·1%	9·0%	**9·4%**
Profit before tax and interest as a percentage of average capital employed	23·9%	31·9%	36·8%	31·9%	**34·7%**
Earnings per 25p share*: basic	6·3p	9·8p	19·3p	24·8p	**34·1p**
fully diluted	6·1p	9·4p	18·3p	23·4p	**32·2p**
Dividend per 25p share*	1·21p	1·33p	1·48p	2·23p	**5·0p**
Number of times covered	4·3	5·9	13·4	11·0	**6·6**
Assets per 25p share*	43p	58p	86p	99p	**123p**

†Not reflecting accounting change re deferred taxation.
*Adjusted for capitalisation issues.

Report of the Auditors

To the Members of British Vita Company Limited

We have examined the accounts set out on pages 15 to 25 and 28.
Incorporated in these accounts are accounts of overseas subsidiaries
and overseas associated companies audited by other firms who have
reported thereon directly to us.
In our opinion the accounts which have been prepared on the
historical cost basis of accounting modified for revaluation of certain
fixed assets give, so far as concerns the members of the Company, a
true and fair view of the state of affairs at 31 December 1979 and of
the profit and source and application of funds for the year ended on
that date and comply with the Companies Acts 1948 and 1967.
We have also examined the current cost accounts set out on pages
26 and 27. In our opinion they have been prepared in accordance
with the bases included in the notes to those accounts.

Huddersfield   C. Connelly
14 March 1980   *Chartered Accountants*

Accounting Policies

1 Basis of consolidation The Group accounts are prepared on a historical cost basis, modified to include the revaluation of certain fixed assets. The Company accounts and those of its United Kingdom and European subsidiaries are made up for a period of 52 weeks ending within or at the end of December. The accounts of the other overseas subsidiaries are made up to 30 September.

Where subsidiaries are acquired or sold during the year the Profit and Loss Account includes the results from the date of acquisition or to the date of sale respectively. On the acquisition of a business, the difference between the consideration paid and the values attributed to the net assets at acquisition is dealt with through reserves.

2 Associated companies The Group accounts include in the Profit and Loss Account the Group's share of the profit of the associated companies after allowing for losses and the Balance Sheet includes the shareholdings at cost and loans to associated companies together with the Group's share of post-acquisition reserves. The accounts used for this purpose are audited accounts for a period ending not more than six months before 31 December, adjusted as appropriate on consolidation to accord with the Group's accounting policies.

3 Deferred taxation is accounted for in respect of the taxation effects of all timing differences of a material amount other than those which can be demonstrated with reasonable probability to continue in the future.

4 Depreciation has been calculated on the full cost price or revalued amounts at rates estimated to write off the assets over their useful lives, annual reviews being made for obsolescence. The main rates generally in use are:
(a) Freehold buildings (excluding land) – $2\frac{1}{2}$% per annum straight line.
(b) Leasehold land and buildings – $2\frac{1}{2}$% per annum straight line or over the period of the lease if less than forty years.
(c) Plant (including fixed plant in buildings) – 10% per annum straight line, but, where the estimated useful life of significant plant is short, a higher rate is used.
(d) Motor vehicles – on a reducing balance or straight line basis at rates between 14% and 30% per annum depending on use.

5 Stocks have been valued at the lower of cost and net realisable value. The value of finished goods and work in progress has been determined by computations which are appropriate to arriving at the costs involved in bringing the products to their current state.

6 Grants on assets are credited to the Profit and Loss Account over the lives of the relevant assets. Other grants are credited to revenue in the year in which the expenditure to which they relate is charged.

7 Research and development, patents and trade marks expenditure is charged against profit of the year in which it is incurred.

8 Foreign currencies are translated at the rates of exchange ruling at the year end. Exchange differences arising from trading transactions, translation losses on foreign currency net borrowings and realised gains on foreign currency borrowings are included in the Profit and Loss Account. Translation gains on foreign currency borrowings and translation differences on fixed assets and arising on consolidation are taken to reserves. Conversion and translation differences arising from realignment of currencies are shown as extraordinary items in the Profit and Loss Account.

9 Comparative figures have been adjusted where necessary to restate the prior year on a comparable basis.

GROUP

Profit and Loss Account
for the year ended 31 December 1979

£000	Notes	1979	1978
Turnover to external customers	1	**73,296**	49,874
Trading profit	2	**6,875**	4,482
Share of profit of associated companies	3	**3,129**	2,793
Interest	4	**(1,076)**	(443)
Profit before tax		**8,928**	6,832
Tax	5	**(2,102)**	(1,923)
Profit after tax		**6,826**	4,909
Minority interests		**(64)**	(20)
Profit before extraordinary items		**6,762**	4,889
Extraordinary items	6	**—**	(30)
Profit attributable to shareholders	7	**6,762**	4,859
Dividends	8	**(1,023)**	(442)
Profit retained for year		**5,739**	4,417
Retained by:			
British Vita Company Limited		**2,805**	2,344
Subsidiary companies		**1,856**	891
Associated companies		**1,078**	1,182
		5,739	4,417
Earnings per share of 25p:	9		
Basic		**34·1p**	24·8p
Fully diluted		**32·2p**	23·4p

Notes on pages 15 and 18 to 23 form part of the Accounts.

Balance Sheets

as at 31 December 1979

£000	Notes	**1979**	1978	**1979**	1978
		Group		**Company**	
Assets employed:					
Fixed assets	11	**17,012**	11,406	**5,488**	2,489
Subsidiaries	12	**—**	—	**10,726**	8,305
Associated companies	13	**8,615**	7,421	**244**	235
Deferred assets	14	**728**	393	**657**	393
Net current assets		**6,379**	5,694	**1,440**	2,288
Stocks	15	**10,190**	7,211	**4,462**	3,242
Debtors		**20,572**	13,006	**11,167**	8,341
Marketable investment	16	**53**	53	**53**	53
Cash and bank balances	10	**1,692**	1,931	**62**	634
		32,507	22,201	**15,744**	12,270
Less:					
Creditors	17	**20,004**	13,132	**12,037**	9,402
Short term borrowings	18	**4,155**	1,539	**1,287**	100
Taxation		**1,426**	1,572	**437**	216
Dividend		**543**	264	**543**	264
		26,128	16,507	**14,304**	9,982
		32,734	24,914	**18,555**	13,710
Capital employed:					
Capital and reserves					
Issued share capital	19	**5,028**	4,175	**5,028**	4,175
Reserves	20	**19,430**	15,416	**8,896**	6,590
		24,458	19,591	**13,924**	10,765
Minority interests in subsidiaries		**265**	102	**—**	—
Loans	21	**6,511**	4,946	**3,476**	2,925
Long term creditors	22	**1,500**	275	**1,155**	20
		32,734	24,914	**18,555**	13,710

F. A. Parker ⎱ *Directors*
R. McGee ⎰

Notes on pages 15 and 18 to 23 form part of the Accounts

Notes on Profit and Loss Account

£000	1979	1978

1 Turnover
This represents the net amounts invoiced to customers in respect of goods supplied and services rendered but excludes value added and sales taxes and any part of the sales of associated companies.

2 Trading profit

	1979	1978
After charging:		
Depreciation†	**1,536**	954
Leasing of vehicles and plant	**468**	354
Directors' emoluments (including pension contributions):		
as directors	**16**	15
as executives	**325**	246
Former directors' pensions and pension contributions	**26**	26
Auditors' remuneration	**90**	62
After crediting:		
Government grants	**45**	21

†New depreciation rates have been adopted in 1979 for specific categories of commercial vehicles. Had the depreciation rates used in 1978 been applied, the depreciation charge for the year would have increased by £134,000.

Directors and UK senior employees
Emoluments (excluding pension contributions)

	1979	1978
Chairman	**£31,000**	£23,814*
Highest paid director	**£41,382**	£36,000

*Appointed 22 March 1978

	Other directors		Employees	
	1979	1978	1979	1978
Below £5,000	**1**	2		
£5,001–£10,000	**1**	1		
£10,001–£15,000	**—**	—		
£15,001–£20,000	**—**	1		
£20,001–£25,000	**3**	3	**1**	—
£25,001–£30,000	**4**	1	**—**	—

3 Associated companies
The appropriate Profit and Loss Account headings include:

	1979	1978
Share of profit *less* losses	**3,129**	2,793
Tax	**(1,104)**	(1,202)
Extraordinary items	**—**	(95)
	2,025	1,496
Receivable as dividends	**(947)**	(314)
Retained by associated companies	**1,078**	1,182

4 Interest

	1979	1978
Bank overdrafts, acceptance credits and bank loans	**829**	238
Loans not fully repayable within five years	**165**	170
Hire purchase and other items	**150**	99
	1,144	507
Less receivable	**(68)**	(64)
	1,076	443

£000	1979	1978
5 Tax		
UK: corporation tax on the profit for the year at 52%	1,140	557
double tax relief	(1,015)	(450)
	125	107
Overseas tax	873	614
Associated companies – tax on share of profit	1,104	1,202
	2,102	1,923

UK tax charge for the year has been reduced by utilisation of brought forward taxation losses (£267,000), accelerated capital allowances (£2,655,000) and stock appreciation relief (£1,568,000). There are UK taxation losses carried forward amounting to £1,028,000.

6 Extraordinary items		
Profit or share of profit on disposal of businesses and assets	—	17
Cost of closures of operations – amount written back	—	6
Overseas subsidiaries – previous provision for loss of goods in transit (net of tax of £50,000) – amount written back	—	50
Overseas associated company – share of unrealised loss on devaluation	—	(103)
	—	(30)

7 Profit available to shareholders		
Amount dealt with in the accounts of British Vita Company Limited	3,828	2,786

8 Dividends		
Ordinary shares:		
Interim – paid 2·4p per share (0·89p)	478	176
Final – proposed 2·6p per share (1·34p)	543	264
Total Ordinary dividends paid and proposed	1,021	440
4·2% Cumulative Preference shares	2	2
	1,023	442

9 Earnings per ordinary share of 25p
The calculation of net earnings per share is based on earnings (after minority interests and Preference dividend but before extraordinary items) of £6,760,000 (£4,887,000) and on 19,847,368 shares (19,725,462 as adjusted for the capitalisation issue) being the weighted average of Ordinary shares in issue during the year. The calculation of fully diluted earnings per share is made on adjusted earnings and shares on the assumptions that all outstanding share options had been exercised and the cash subscribed on the exercise of the options had been invested throughout the year at a rate equivalent to the yield on 2½% Consols at the opening Balance Sheet date.

10 Remittances from overseas subsidiary and associated companies
The dividends received in the UK during the year were £897,000 (£555,000). The reserves of overseas subsidiary and associated companies if distributed as dividends would be liable to overseas taxes and, subject to double tax relief, UK taxation. As no such distributions are likely in the foreseeable future, no provision has been made. There are exchange control restrictions in certain overseas countries on the remittance of funds to the United Kingdom. In particular in Zambia as at 31 December 1979 dividends for 1978 of £220,000 and trading account indebtedness of £316,000 had been paid into the Standard Bank of Zambia Limited but awaited remittance approval. These sums are included in the cash and bank balances in the Group Balance Sheet.

Notes on Balance Sheets

£000

11 Fixed assets

	Group		Company
	Land and buildings	Plant, equipment and vehicles	Plant, equipment and vehicles
Cost and valuation			
Balance 31 December 1978	7,082	12,543	7,161
Exchange rate adjustment	(97)	1	—
Additions	518	4,766	3,645
Inter Group transfers	—	—	5
New subsidiaries	1,217	3,540	—
Disposals	—	(643)	(49)
Revaluation†	67	—	—
Balance 31 December 1979	8,787	20,207	10,762
Accumulated depreciation			
Balance 31 December 1978	358	7,861	4,672
Exchange rate adjustment	4	—	—
Inter Group transfers	—	—	3
New subsidiaries	341	2,370	—
Charge for year	251	1,285	628
Disposals	—	(477)	(29)
Written back on revaluation†	(11)	—	—
Balance 31 December 1979	943	11,039	5,274
Net book value analysis			
Valuation: 1970	287	—	—
1976	281	—	—
1977	3,336	—	—
1978	1,700	—	—
1979	1,044	—	—
Cost	1,196	9,168	5,488
	7,844	9,168	
Per Balance Sheets		17,012	5,488
Land and buildings comprise:			
Freehold	6,688		
Long leasehold	1,058		
Short leasehold	98		
	7,844		

No provision is made for capital gains tax which might arise on disposal at book values of properties which in the main are held for long term use in the Group's business.

†During the year, part of the long leasehold land and buildings of a Zambian subsidiary were independently valued on a current market value basis by J. W. Robertson, FRICS.

12 Subsidiaries

	Company	
	1979	1978
Shares at cost *less* amounts written off	5,387	3,981
Amounts owed to dormant subsidiaries	(992)	(992)
	4,395	2,989
Amounts owed by operating subsidiaries	6,331	5,316
	10,726	8,305

£000	1979	1978	1979	1978
	Group		Company	

13 Associated companies
Unlisted investments

	1979	1978	1979	1978
Shares at cost	1,427	1,125	232	223
Share of post-acquisition reserves	3,205	2,117	—	—
	4,632	3,242	232	223

Directors' valuation £6,300,000 (£4,846,000) for the Group
and £750,000 (£500,000) for the Company.

Listed investment – overseas

	1979	1978	1979	1978
Shares at cost	20	20	—	—
Share of post-acquisition reserves	3,555	3,431	—	—
Market value £2,738,000 (£2,154,000)	3,575	3,451	—	—
Loans	408	728	12	12
	8,615	7,421	244	235

14 Deferred assets

	1979	1978	1979	1978
Amount due from sale of assets and goodwill	189	221	189	221
ACT recoverable	468	172	468	172
Interest relief grants and deposits receivable	71	—	—	—
	728	393	657	393

15 Stocks

	1979	1978	1979	1978
Raw materials and consumable stores	8,118	5,795	3,669	2,596
Work in progress and finished goods	2,072	1,416	793	646
	10,190	7,211	4,462	3,242

16 Marketable investment

	1979	1978	1979	1978
Listed – at cost (market value £153,000) (£141,000)	53	53	53	53

17 Creditors

	1979	1978	1979	1978
Trade and other creditors	19,577	12,954	11,713	9,356
Proportion of long term creditors (note 22)	427	178	324	46
	20,004	13,132	12,037	9,402

18 Short term borrowings (repayable within one year or on demand)

	1979	1978	1979	1978
Bank overdrafts: unsecured	1,758	628	1,187	—
secured	1,505	299	—	—
Proportion of loans (note 21)	892	612	100	100
	4,155	1,539	1,287	100

19 Share capital

	Authorised		Issued and fully paid	
	1979	1978	1979	1978
4·2% Cumulative Preference shares of £1 each	60	60	57	57
Ordinary shares of 25p each	7,000	5,000	4,971	4,118
	7,060	5,060	5,028	4,175

Options outstanding under the Company's share option schemes
as at 31 December 1979 are shown on page 11.

£000

20 Reserves	Group	Company
Company and subsidiaries		
Balance 31 December 1978	9,868	6,590
Transfer from subsidiaries	—	318
Surplus on revaluation of property	78	—
Capitalisation issue	(823)	(823)
Share premium on share options exercised	14	14
Share option capitalisation	(19)	(19)
Goodwill on acquisition	(870)	—
Exchange adjustments and miscellaneous	(239)	11
Retained profit	4,661	2,805
	12,670	8,896
Associated companies		
Balance 31 December 1978	5,548	
Surplus on revaluation of fixed assets	304	
Exchange adjustments and miscellaneous	(170)	
Retained profit	1,078 6,760	
	19,430	8,896

Included in the Company and subsidiaries reserves above are:
Deficit arising on consolidation £1,026,000 (£81,000).
Share premium account – Group £16,000 (£10,000),
Company £14,000 (£8,000).
Capital redemption fund – Group £12,000 (£12,000).
Share option capitalisation reserve – Company £199,000 (£150,000)

	Group		Company	
21 Loans	1979	1978	1979	1978
Long term (not wholly repayable within 5 years)				
UK: 7¼% debenture stock 1987/92	547	575	547	575
10¼% debenture stock 1990/95	1,000	1,000	1,000	1,000
Bank loan 1980/85	1,100	1,200	1,100	1,200
Overseas: 9½% and 12% mortgages 1980/87	224	249		
Bf bank loans 1980/89	2,370	—		
Medium term (repayable within 5 years)				
UK: Bank loan 1981/83	750	250	750	250
Bf bank loan 1982	160	—	160	
US and Can dollar bank loans 1980/84	285	998		
Dfl bank loans 1980/83	493	914	19	—
8½% mortgage debenture	—	4		
Overseas: Dfl bank loan 1980/81	474	368		
	7,403	5,558	3,576	3,025
Less short term proportion included in short term borrowings (note 18)	(892)	(612)	(100)	(100)
	6,511	4,946	3,476	2,925

Interest charges on the bank loans are linked to inter-bank rates relative
to the currency borrowed. All loans are secured other than UK bank loans.

The loans are repayable as follows:				
Between one and two years	910	453	425	100
Between two and five years	2,589	2,247	1,304	850
In five years or more	3,012	2,246	1,747	1,975
	6,511	4,946	3,476	2,925
22 Long term creditors				
Hire purchase	1,687	430	1,395	43
Government grants	240	23	84	23
	1,927	453	1,479	66
Less short term proportion included in creditors (note 17)	(427)	(178)	(324)	(46)
	1,500	275	1,155	20

£000

23 Deferred taxation

Applying the Group accounting policy no provision is required for deferred taxation. The amounts of UK deferred taxation not provided for in the accounts computed on the liability method and expressed in terms of a 52% corporation tax rate are set out below:

	Group		Company	
	1979	1978	**1979**	1978
Stock appreciation relief	**1,604**	787	**1,056**	612
Accelerated capital allowances	**3,930**	2,402	**2,496**	1,294
Miscellaneous	**—**	49	**—**	—
	5,534	3,238	**3,552**	1,906

There are ACT credits carried forward in both Group and Company of £587,000 (£293,000).

24 Pensions

In the UK, contributions at rates recommended by actuaries and reviewed biennially, are made to funded schemes. The assets of the funds are held by a trust company, British Vita Pensions Trust Limited, and are kept separate from those of the Group. The Company is funding increased pensions to existing pensioners from 6 April 1980 at a capital cost of £73,660. An equivalent percentage pension increase is being paid by the Company in respect of non-funded pensions at an annual cost of £1,830. Provision for these sums has been made in the accounts to 31 December 1979.

A UK subsidiary has a contingent liability referable to past service in connection with pension funding. The estimated amount of this liability at 31 December 1979 was £80,000 and will be met over the next nine years.

25 Contingent liabilities

The Company has guaranteed certain of the overdrafts and third party liabilities of certain of its subsidiary companies, amounting to £1,447,000 (£1,067,000).

There are contingent liabilities in connection with legal claims and bills of exchange the ascertainable amount of which was £262,000 (£40,700) for the Group and £154,000 (£14,700) for the Company.

The Company has guaranteed borrowings under bank facilities amounting to £298,000 (£274,000) for certain associated companies.

The Company has issued a guarantee in the maximum sum of £50,000 (£50,000) in respect of part of the obligations of one overseas associated company for the purchase of UK capital equipment.

The Company with others and with the benefit of cross indemnities has issued a joint and several guarantee amounting to £228,000 (£184,000) for working capital finance for an associated company.

26 Capital commitments

Commitments for capital expenditure at 31 December 1979 not provided for in the accounts amounted to £1,987,000 (£898,000) for the Group and £877,000 (£573,000) for the Company. In addition capital expenditure authorised by the directors but not contracted amounted to £748,000 (£966,000) for the Group and £181,000 (£488,000) for the Company.

Subsidiary Companies

The ordinary share capital of these companies is wholly owned by British Vita Company Limited, except as otherwise indicated. The companies are incorporated and operate in the countries indicated. The overseas companies are held directly by Vita International Limited or, where marked with an asterisk, through subsidiary companies. Particulars of certain subsidiaries, none of which are material in relation to the Profit and Loss Account and Balance Sheets, are omitted and will be included in the annual return.

	Country	Products or activities
United Kingdom		
Blue Dart Transport Limited	England	Haulage contracting
British Vita Company (Engineering) Limited	England	Engineering services
British Vita Investments Limited	England	Property management
Caligen Foam Limited	England	Cellular foam products
Chemibond Limited	England	Merchanting
Foam Components Limited	England	Cellular foam products
Portways Limited	England	Fibre fillings and related consumer products
Vita International Limited	England	Co-ordination of overseas interests
Europe		
Caligen Europe BV* Breda	Netherlands	Cellular foam products
Libeltex NV* Meulebeke	Belgium	Fibre processing
Vita Polymers Europe BV The Hague	Netherlands	Holding company
Vitafoam Europe BV* The Hague	Netherlands	Holding company
International		
Furniture Corporation of Zambia Limited (95%) Ndola	Zambia	Furniture, mattresses and retailing
South African Vita (Pty) Limited (90%)* Benoni	South Africa	Fabric coating
Vitafoam Kenya Limited (see page 9) Nairobi, Mombasa and Kisumu	Kenya	Cellular foam products
Vitafoam Zambia Limited (95%) Ndola	Zambia	Cellular foam products and fabric coating

Associated Companies

All companies are held directly or indirectly by Vita International Limited except for BTR-Vitaline and Somercel Limited which are held by British Vita Company Limited. Their principal activity is the manufacture of cellular foam products except for BTR-Vitaline Limited (rubber lining of tanks), Somercel Limited (holding company of Hairlok Limited which manufactures cellular foam and rubberised curled hair products) and Sodico SA (moulded plastic products). Vita Cortex Limited also processes fibres through its subsidiary Vitabond Limited.

Country of incorporation and principal operation	Name	Equity Total Interest 000's	Company %	Loans Total Interest 000's	Company %	Results up to
United Kingdom and Europe						
England	BTR-Vitaline Limited	£50	50·0	—	—	31 December
England	Somercel Limited	£476	44·0	£94	12·8	31 December
Ireland	Vita Cortex Limited	I£529	50·0	—	—	31 December
International						
Australia	Vitafoam Australia Pty Limited	A$11	40·0	A$300	—	30 June
Barbados	Vitafoam Barbados Limited	B$75	50·0	—	—	30 September
Canada	Vitafoam Products Canada Limited	C$20	50·0	C$1,472	23·0	30 September
Central African Republic	Vita Centrafrique SA	CFA12,000	50·0	CFA48,000	55·0	See note 3
Egypt	Taki-Vita SAE	E£2,000	40·0	E£3,422	14·3	31 December
Fiji	Vitafoam Fiji Limited	F$18	45·0	F$92	80·0	30 September
Fiji	Hensher (Fiji) Limited	F$9	45·0	—	—	30 September
Indonesia	PT Vitafoam Indonesia	Rup273,900	37·5	Rup756,250	12·3	30 September
Japan	Vita Colourfoam Japan Limited	¥30,000	20·0	¥240,000	—	30 June
Malagasy	Vitafoam Madagascar SA	Fmg24,000	41·7	—	—	31 December
Malta	Vitafoam Limited	M£50	50·0	M£12	—	31 December
Nigeria	Vitafoam Nigeria Limited	N13,650	20·0	N6	50·0	30 September
Reunion	Isoplast SARL	F Fr730	22·8	—	—	30 June
Reunion	Sodico SA	F Fr1,025	29·3	—	—	30 June
South Africa	Vitafoam SA (Pty) Limited	R150	50·0	—	—	31 December
Sudan	Vitaprene Sudan Limited	S£20	50·0	S£35	50·0	See note 4
Trinidad	Vitafoam Trinidad Limited	TT $300	40·0	—	—	31 October
Uganda	Vitafoam Uganda Limited	U.Shs200	50·0	—	—	See note 4

Notes

1 Associated companies' holdings of issued capital of other companies include:
Somercel Limited—100% of Hairlok Limited and its subsidiaries;
Vita Cortex Limited—100% of Vita Cortex (Dublin) Limited, Vita Cortex (Navan) Limited, Vita Cortex (NI) Limited and Vitabond Limited;
Vitafoam Australia Pty Limited—*25% of Vita Colourfoam Japan Limited, 24·9% of Vitafoam New Zealand Limited and 50% of Vita Monier (PNG) Limited;
Isoplast SARL—*27% of Sodico SA;
Vitafoam SA (Pty) Limited—100% of Vitafoam CA (Private) Limited.
* Excluded from Company Interest % in table above.

2 Vita International Limited also holds 50% of the C$180,000 preference shares of Vitafoam Products Canada Limited which itself has a substantial interest in the ordinary share capital of Vitafoam Midwest Limited.

3 Vita Centrafrique SA commenced trading during the year and the first results will be to 30 June 1980.

4 As audited accounts of Vitaprene Sudan Limited and Vitafoam Uganda Limited have not yet been received, their results, which are not considered to be material, are not included.

Current Cost Accounts

£000		Notes	1979

The accounts have been prepared in accordance with the proposed statement of standard accounting practice on Current Cost Accounting (ED24) issued by the Accounting Standards Committee.

Current Cost Profit and Loss Account
for the year ended 31 December 1979

	Notes	1979
Turnover		73,296
Trading profit	2	3,467
Share of profit of associated companies	1(b)	3,129
Interest		(1,076)
Gearing adjustment	1(a)	851
Profit before tax		6,371
Tax		(2,102)
Minority interests		(64)
Profit attributable to shareholders		4,205
Dividends		(1,023)
Profit retained for year		3,182
Earnings per share (basic)	3	21·2p

Summarised Current Cost Group Balance Sheet
as at 31 December 1979

Assets employed	Notes	
Fixed assets	4	26,372
Associated companies	1(b)	8,615
Deferred assets		728
Net current assets		6,615
Current assets		32,743
Current liabilities		26,128
		42,330
Capital employed		
Issued share capital		5,028
Reserves	5	29,026
		34,054
Minority interests in subsidiaries		265
Loans		6,511
Long term creditors		1,500
		42,330

£000

---

1 Accounting policies (in so far as they differ from those set out on page 15 for the historical cost accounts)

(a) **Basis**—the Group's results on an historical cost basis have been adjusted to reflect the value to the business of fixed assets and stocks consumed during the year, and to take account of additional finance required for monetary working capital. A gearing adjustment has also been made which reduces the current cost adjustments by the proportion which has been financed by borrowings.

(b) **Associated companies**—no adjustments have been made in respect of the Group's investments in and share of profit of associated companies as the information required to restate the figures is not readily available.

(c) **Stocks** are valued at the lower of current cost replacement and net realisable value.

(d) **Cost of sales adjustment**—an adjustment, using the averaging method, has been made in the case of stocks consumed during the year to take account of the increased cost of purchasing and manufacturing replacement stocks at the costs current at the time of consumption. This has been calculated by reference to indices appropriate to the company concerned.

(e) **Monetary working capital adjustment**—an adjustment has been made to take account of the amount of additional finance required during the year for monetary working capital as a result of changes in prices, and has been calculated on the averaging method by reference to indices appropriate to the company concerned.

(f) **Depreciation**—adjustment represents the excess of the depreciation calculated on the inflation-adjusted cost of fixed assets over the depreciation charged in the historical cost accounts.

2 Trading profit

Historical trading profit		6,875
Current cost adjustments:		
Cost of sales	(1,168)	
Monetary working capital	(467)	
Depreciation	(1,773)	(3,408)
		———
Current cost trading profit		3,467

3 Earnings per share—the calculation of net current cost earnings per share is based on adjusted earnings of £4,203,000 and 19,847,368 shares.

4 Fixed assets—are included at net current replacement values based on professional valuations or cost adjusted by reference to indices appropriate to the company concerned.

5 Reserves—the adjustments referred to above have been transferred to a capital maintenance reserve, the balance of which of £12,153,000 represents the amount required by the Group to maintain the operating capacity of its business, to the extent that this has not already been allowed for in the historical cost accounts.

Source and Application of Funds

£000		1979		1978
Source of funds				
Profit before tax and extraordinary items *less* minority interests		**8,864**		6,812
Extraordinary items		**—**		(30)
Disposal of fixed assets		**166**		493
		9,030		7,275
Items not involving the movement of funds				
Minority interests in the retained profit of the year		**64**		20
Depreciation and plant obsolescence		**1,536**		954
Profit retained in associated companies		**(1,078)**		(1,182)
Total funds generated from operations		**9,552**		7,067
Use of funds				
Dividends paid and proposed	**1,023**		442	
Tax on the profit of the year	**2,102**		1,923	
Purchase of fixed assets	**5,284**		2,046	
Purchase of new subsidiaries (Note)	**2,714**		2,000	
Investment in associated companies	**(18)**		344	
Debentures redeemed	**28**		25	
Increase in deferred assets	**253**		107	
Other items	**39**		74	
Working capital movement				
Increase in stocks	**1,657**		929	
Increase in debtors	**4,710**		463	
Increase in creditors	**(4,768)**	**13,024**	(1,530)	6,823
Additional funding requirement/(generated)		**3,472**		(244)
How financed				
Increase in loans		**617**		391
Increase in long term creditors		**1,225**		—
Issue of ordinary share capital under share option schemes		**24**		12
Decrease/(increase) in net cash balances		**1,606**		(647)
Total financing		**3,472**		(244)

Note—Analysis of the acquisition of subsidiaries

	1979	1978
Net assets acquired:		
Fixed assets	**2,046**	2,507
Deferred assets	**82**	—
Current assets	**4,404**	2,648
Current liabilities	**(3,712)**	(2,340)
Loans	**(976)**	(1,034)
Net tangible assets	**1,844**	1,781
Goodwill on acquisition	**870**	219
	2,714	2,000
Discharged by:		
Cash paid	**2,658**	1,500
Cash payable	**56**	500
	2,714	2,000

Statement of Value Added

£000	1979	1978

Value added is a measure of the amount of wealth that British Vita and its subsidiaries create by their activities. This statement and diagram show how the value added has been shared amongst those contributing to its creation and paid to governments for taxation.

	1979	1978
Turnover including taxes	81,173	54,763
Less materials and services including taxes	(51,648)	(35,041)
Value added	**29,525**	19,722
Applied as follows:		
To personnel for wages, salaries, pension and social security contributions	16,662	11,632
To governments for taxation	4,625	3,106
To providers of capital:		
interest on loans	1,018	353
dividends to shareholders	1,023	442
To provide for maintenance of assets and expansion:		
depreciation	1,536	954
retained earnings	4,661	3,235
	29,525	19,722

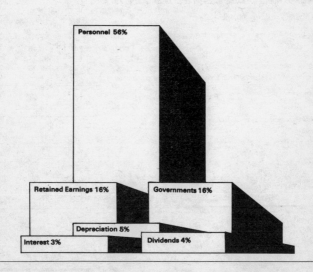

Shareholding Information

Financial calendar

Preliminary announcement of results for year	Early March
Report and Accounts circulated	Late March
Annual General Meeting	Mid April
Interim Report	Early September

Dividend payments

Ordinary shares: Interim	Early November
Final	Early May
Preference shares	31 March and 30 September

Interest payments

$7\frac{1}{2}$% Debenture Stock	31 March and 30 September
$10\frac{1}{4}$% Debenture Stock	30 June and 31 December
Loan Notes	31 January, 30 April, 31 July and 31 October

Ordinary share ownership analysis at 31 December 1979

	Number of holdings	Shares Number	%
Individuals 1–1,000	1,261	576,463	2·9
1,001–10,000	1,112	2,590,343	13·0
over 10,000	96	5,029,401	25·3
Trusts, pension funds and insurance companies	76	8,124,614	40·9
Unit trusts and investment companies	28	839,797	4·2
Banks and nominee companies	120	2,409,699	12·1
Others	48	312,395	1·6
	2,741	19,882,712	100·0

Printed by Watmoughs Limited, Idle, Bradford; and London

Appendix D *British Vita Interim Statement 1980*

Chairman's Review

Your Company, its subsidiaries and associates have made a Profit before tax of £3.67 million (£4.05 million) for the half year to 30th June, 1980. Of this total profit £1.66 million (£2.25 million) arises from the operations in the UK and Europe and £2.01 (£1.80 million) from International. Earnings per share are being affected by the reduced Profit before tax and the Group's increasing liability to UK Corporation Tax.

On 5th February, 1980 the Company acquired Vita-tex Limited, textile processors specialising in the printing, dyeing, laminating and finishing of textiles for a variety of purposes. This acquisition is not only making a satisfactory contribution to Group profitability but has also extended and complemented the technology of the Group and its ability to manufacture additional products.

Since I last reported on the position of the Group at the Annual General Meeting in April the recession in the UK further deepened during May and June. Currently the very high levels of unemployment and the uncertainty of the British economy make it difficult to be optimistic about the immediate future of UK industry. Your Board and management, having anticipated the situation, took early action to contain the problems being forced on the Group. In particular stock levels have been reduced and there has had to be a reduction in both staff and works personnel in order to contain overheads and match costs to levels of production.

Your Group's immediate prospects in the UK and Europe must be looked at with some caution and it would not be prudent for the Board to make a forecast for the remainder of the year other than to say that in common with most sectors of industry pre-tax profit margins must inevitably be reduced by the recession, by the high interest rates and by the strength of sterling. Performance in the UK particularly is being affected by the depressed state of the furniture and automotive industries. Nevertheless, the Group continues to enjoy its traditional strength in the markets it serves and, by reason of its recent acquisitions, its development programme and the renewal of assets to meet current technological requirements, it is well placed to take advantage of any improvement in economic conditions.

The Group's International operations show a profit for the first half of the year ahead of that for the same period last year. I stated in my Review included with the 1979 Report and Accounts that the International profit for the second half of last year included some element that arose from non-recurring contracts. While overall no increase in demand is anticipated in the second half of 1980, margins are being maintained at generally satisfactory levels.

Your Board are convinced that whilst a policy of conserving existing resources must continue, they should nevertheless maintain their strategy of investing both through acquisition and direct capital expenditure in projects which widen and strengthen the Group's base at home and overseas.

Your Board have declared an Interim Dividend on the Ordinary Shares of 2.6p per share (1979 – 2.4 p) payable on 3rd November, 1980 to Ordinary Shareholders on the register at the close of business on 3rd October, 1980.

10th September, 1980

F. A. Carter

International leaders in foams, fibre

Group Interim Results
(unaudited) for the six months ended 30th June 1980

Year 1979	£000	First Half 1980	1979
73,296	**Turnover to external customers**	**46,552**	31,702
6,875	**Trading profit**	**3,193**	3,063
3,129	**Share of profit of associated companies**	**1,528**	1,373
(1,076)	**Interest**	**(1,050)**	(381)
8,928	**Profit before tax**	**3,671**	4,055
4,593	United Kingdom and Europe	1,663	2,252
4,335	International	2,008	1,803
(2,102)	**Tax – estimated**	**(1,414)**	(1,035)
6,826	**Profit after tax**	**2,257**	3,020
(64)	**Minority interests**	**(29)**	(36)
–	**Extraordinary items**	**110**	–
6,762	**Profit attributable to shareholders**	**2,338**	2,984
1,023	**Cost of dividends**	**551**	478
	Earnings per share of 25p:		
34.1p	Basic	**10.7p**	15.1p
32.2p	Fully diluted	**10.3p**	14.3p
5.0p	**Dividend per share of 25p**	**2.6p**	2.4p

brics and rubber technology

Index

(Note: Appendixes B, C and D have not been indexed.)